Chuck Faulkner's 750 Helpful Household Hints

Donning
Norfolk/Virginia Beach

The Donning Company/Publishers,
5659 Virginia Beach Boulevard
Norfolk, Virginia 23502

Library of Congress Cataloging in Publication Data

Faulkner, Charles S.
    750 helpful household hints.

    1. Home economics.   I. Title.
TX158.F35   1982   640   82-19820
ISBN 0-89865-262-6

Printed in the United States of America

To Charles IV and Julie
"Two Beautiful People"!
With Love

750 Helpful Household Hints

To
The Reader

When I started collecting hints nearly a half century ago, I little dreamed that in 1982 this book would be the result.

The very first hint came from my mother, who always melted (caramelized) a dessert-spoonful of sugar over our open stove fire before adding it to the evening stew, casserole, or soup. "Improves the flavor," she'd tell me, and it always did.

I remember my sister walking around the house, rubbing half a raw potato on her face. When I finally asked her why, I was politely informed, "Best thing in the world for blackheads and rashes," and she was right.

After a hard soccer match, my father would immerse himself in a tub of hot water into which he'd sprinkled a half cup of Epsom salts. Keeping the water hot by slowly running the tap, he'd splash like a seal for fifteen or twenty minutes, then emerge as red as a lobster. "Great for tired muscles and bones," he'd tell me. "Don't forget it, son!" My father is still alive today, nearly ninety years of age, and is in far better condition than I am.

The advice I may have forgotten, but not the hints. I've been collecting them ever since. Scraps of paper, postcards, letters—not to mention thousands of phone calls from friends, relatives, and my radio listeners—were finally sorted out, indexed, and typed. The 750 hints in this edition are only a small section of them, which I hope will lead to a later second edition.

It would be very lax of me if I didn't take this opportunity to offer a sincere thank you to the thousands of WNIS radio listeners who have unhesitatingly given me their family hints over the past two-and-a-half years. I'd only have to admit that I had no idea how to get rid of mice, when some listener would telephone me and give me an old family remedy. Two of the best, I learned, are fresh mint squeezed in the hand, then scattered around the area, and, surprisingly, powdered cinnamon sprinkled around the cupboards and shelves. Some of the hints that were called in or written and sent in date back over 100 years and are as good today as they were a century ago.

I'd also like to thank my good friends and relatives, scattered around the world, who (knowing my hobby as well as my "cooking and hint" radio show) have never faulted in discovering new hints and forwarding them to me from such distant places as Belfast (Ireland), Sydney and Melbourne (Australia), Montreal (Canada), and Los Angeles (USA). Without them, this book could not have been written.

No household hint is infallible! Where one hint will prove an instant success in one household, negative results may occur in a second residence. Don't ask why. Maybe it's the wrong flour (self-rising instead of plain, perhaps); a long-opened bottle of hydrogen peroxide (with little fizz) could have been used instead of a fresh one; or rubbing alcohol is substituted for denatured alcohol. The reasons may be many, the solutions may escape me.

However, while not guaranteeing any hint in these pages to be one hundred percent infallible,

I can claim a success rate of between ninety and ninety-seven percent over the years—and I hope you have the same success.

Surprisingly, I often find that a new hint which fails to give the desired results the first time will often work perfectly the second time. So don't give up after one trial.

Enjoy reading it. A copy at hand in the kitchen should aid you when those vexing little household problems arise.

Chuck Faulkner
Norfolk, Virginia

Acetone, In Nail Polish Remover

Nail polish remover contains acetone, which will dissolve some materials. Be sure to check the material label before using it.

Acrylics, Machine Washing

Never use hot water. Always wash acrylics in cold water and two teaspoons of any liquid fabric softener. After washing, do not spin dry, but remove carefully, rolling them up. Then hang them in the open air to dry.

Alcohol Stains, Removing

If the stains are fresh (wet), run cold water through the fabric, working it between the fingers. This method of stain removal is good for red or white wines, as well as beer, whiskey, and rum.

If it is an old, dry stain, soak it in white vinegar for fifteen minutes, then sprinkle a powdered detergent on the stain and vigorously rub the spot. Now, wash the item in hot, sudsy water. If the stain remains visible, repeat the process.

Or sponge the stain with turpentine. Work it between the fingers, then hand wash it in warm, sudsy water.

Almonds, Blanching

Place almonds in a pan and cover them with cold water. Bring to a boil, strain them, then run cold water over them. Strain them again and rub with a hand towel or cloth. The skins will come off easily.

Aluminum, Cleaning

Wash the item in warm water to which one cup of vinegar has been added. Next, apply a paste of whiting and water, rub hard, then polish.

Or if the item is badly discolored, fill the pot or pan three-fourths full of water and add some apple parings. Bring slowly to a boil and allow to boil for fifteen minutes. This really works.

Another method is to vigorously rub the pot or pan with a soft cloth which has been dipped in pure lemon juice. When the item is dry, polish it with another soft cloth.

If the pan is badly stained, add three tablespoons of cream of tartar to one quart of water, then boil vigorously for ten minutes.

If using an aluminum double boiler, add one teaspoon of white vinegar to the boiling water in the bottom to improve the taste of food and prevent discoloration of the container.

Aluminum, Preventing Darkening

When cooking eggs, rice, or beans, add about two teaspoons of white vinegar to the water to stop formation of those nasty dark stains.

Aluminum Kettles, Preserving

Always turn them upside down and empty them at night. A good place to do this is in the dishrack. It prevents the bottom of the kettle from rusting inside and it will prevent leaks.

Aluminum Siding, Cleaning

Whether the siding is painted or unpainted, try this: Mix together equal parts of clean motor oil and kerosene. Using a large strip of fine bronze wool, which you can buy at the hardware store, clean the entire surface. Wipe clean with a soft cloth. To prevent further dirt, grease, and grime, next go over the surface with another soft cloth, dipped in the same mixture and wrung out.

Or scrub siding with a mixture of one-half cup of any dishwashing powder to each gallon of hot water. After scrubbing well with a brush or the end of a broom, be sure to rinse thoroughly with clean, cold water.

Angora, Stopping Shedding

Wrap the article (sweater, jacket, scarf) in tissue paper (blue, if possible) and put it in the refrigerator for at least two hours.

Ants, Getting Rid Of

If you can locate the ant hills by following the trail of the ants, pour boiling water down each hole.

If ants are inside, whole cloves scattered around the area are a good ant deterrent.

If ants are a problem outside, any old coffee grounds scattered around your doorsteps, windows, and elsewhere will stop ants in their tracks.

Ants, Keeping Them Away

Mix together three parts powdered borax, one part boric acid, and one part white sugar, then heap one teaspoon in each corner, as well as in any entry spots you happen to find.

Or for a safe and sure method, sprinkle powdered cinnamon in the area.

Using fresh cucumber peelings is also recommended.

If the problem is outside, dissolve one-half pound of aluminum in one quart of boiling water and, using the mixture, scrub your steps, porch, or patio by hand or with the end of a stiff broom.

If the problems is indoors, soak a sponge in very sugary water, then place it in a saucer and let it sit. When the ants cover the sponge, plunge it into boiling water. Keep repeating the process and soon you will have no more ants.

Aphids, Getting Rid Of

A good lukewarm, soapy solution is excellent. Either spray or dip the plants in the soapy water.

If the aphids are on your squash, try putting strips of aluminum foil between the rows. Either lay the foil on the ground, holding it down with small stones, or hang it from garden stakes on a bit of string. Believe it or not, it works.

Or you can soak some old cigarette or cigar butts in water and let it stand for three hours. The stronger, the better. Now, strain, add a little liquid detergent, and either dip or spray the plants.

Note: This method is also good for indoor plants. Depending on the plant size, pour one-half cup to one cup into the soil.

Apples, Bursting While Baking

Prick apples two or three times with a fork before placing them in the oven and their skins will stay whole.

Apples, Preventing Darkening

After paring, dip the apple, or apple pieces, in pure lemon juice. This gives them an especially good flavor as well.

Apple Pie Crust

Try adding a little grated (mild) cheddar cheese to the dough for a marvelous taste.

Artificial Flowers, Cleaning

Put the flowers, either singly or in a bunch, in a brown paper bag, then add one cup of salt. Shake the bag vigorously for thirty seconds. Remove the flowers and shake them over the sink for a few seconds.

Or hold them over a fast boiling kettle for fifteen to thirty seconds to restore their original luster.

Arthritis

There is no known cure for arthritis, but here are a few tips that may help you.

Take a mixture of one tablespoon of Certo (a fruit pectin) and one cup of pure grape juice two to three times a day.

One tablespoon of cod liver oil twice a day is another well-known tip for arthritis sufferers.

Note: For those who don't like the taste, cod liver oil is now available in capsules.

Ashtrays, Cleaning

After washing and drying your ashtray, wax the inside with floor polish or car polish. This will save a lot of washing because it can be readily cleaned out with a paper towel. This is an excellent procedure to use if you're having a party.

Ashtray Gum, Removing

Those hard black stains will come off easily if you soak them with denatured alcohol. Let it soak for two to three minutes, then wash it the normal way.

Asparagus, Keeping It Fresh

Simply stand asparagus in clean, cold water so
that the stalks, not the heads, are half-covered.
They'll keep for weeks in your refrigerator.

B

Baby's Glass, Preventing It From Slipping

If the glass keeps slipping out of the tot's hand,
try stretching two rubber bands around the
glass, about an inch or two from the bottom. It
works.

Bacon, Preventing It From Curling

One of the simplest things to do is to score the
edge of the bacon with a sharp knife, making
nicks about one-half inch apart. This will keep
the bacon flat while it's cooking.

Bacon, Retaining Its Flavor

Bacon is sensitive to cold and will lose its flavor
and aroma if kept in the refrigerator longer than
seven to eight days. If you must keep it longer,
remove it from its package and wrap it
completely in a soft cloth soaked in white
vinegar. It will keep much longer.

Baking Dish, Removing Brown Stains

Soak the dish overnight in a gallon of warm water to which you've added two cups of powdered borax. Next morning, wash in the usual way.

Baking Powder, Making Your Own

Mix together two tablespoons of cream of tartar, one tablespoon of baking soda, and one tablespoon of cornstarch. This will make about eight teaspoons of baking powder.

Bananas, Preserving

First, peel them, then stand them on end in a glass jar. Seal it thoroughly and put it in the refrigerator. They'll keep for weeks.

Bee Sting

Put a slice of raw onion directly onto the affected area and hold it on with tape or cloth.

Or rub tobacco juice directly onto the spot.

Beef, Cleaning

Never use water to clean beef. It will toughen it and ruin the taste. The best thing to use is a soft cloth soaked in white vinegar.

Beef, Keeping It Tender

Soaking it in equal parts of vinegar and water for ten minutes makes it lovely and tender.

Beef, Stewed

A few small onions plus two teaspoons of brown sugar will improve the flavor.

Beetles, Keeping Them Away

Sprinkle a mixture of three parts powdered borax and one part boric acid around the area, particularly along the floorboards and near doors. You might also try heaping a teaspoon in each corner of your room.

Beetles (Japanese), Getting Rid Of
See Japanese Beetles, Getting Rid Of

Beets, Removing Skins Easily

Immediately after boiling them, place them on the end of a fork and dip them into very cold water. The skin can be removed easily.

Bell Peppers, Freezing

Cut the peppers in half, then remove all seeds, core and membranes. Lay the halves on a flat tray, or something similar, making sure the pieces are not touching. After they have frozen, remove them from the freezer, put them in airtight freezing bags, and return them to the freezer.

Biscuits

Any biscuit mixture will improve simply by kneading the dough for one minute after normal mixing.

Biscuit Divider

After kneading and rolling the dough, press a divider from an ice cube tray into the dough. About one-half way into the dough is far enough. After baking, the biscuits will separate easily.

Blackboard Eraser, Substitution

A clean old powder puff is excellent for the task and it's easily washed when soiled.

Blackheads, Removing

If you suffer from blackheads, pimples, shaving rash, try rubbing half a fresh, raw potato on the affected area. The juice of the potato rubbed regularly on the spots seems to work.

Bleach, Substitution

If washing clothes by hand, a half cup of turpentine or kerosene added to very hot water is a good bleaching substitute.

Blind Boil

Those nasty little red lumps will quickly disappear if rubbed with half a fresh lemon. Rub the pulp directly onto the red area.

Blood Stains, Removing

If the stain is fresh (moist), run it under the cold water tap and, as the water runs through the cloth, work it between the fingers.

Note: Never use hot water.

If the blood stain is hard and dry, soak it in cold water to which you have added one teaspoon of baking soda. Soak for at least one hour, working the material between the fingers from time to time. Now, wash in the usual way.

Note: A touch of bleach will finish the job if a dark spot remains. Then hang the item in the sunshine.

If the stain is dry and black, soak it in one gallon of lukewarm water to which you've added one-half cup of ammonia. After thirty minutes, remove and wash in warm, soapy water.

Still another method is to wet the stain with cold water, then sprinkle meat tenderizer onto the material, working it between the fingers for three to five minutes. Then wash the item in cold, sudsy water.

Boilovers, On The Stove Or In The Oven

Cover the boilover immediately with salt. It stops the smoking right away. It also removes all unpleasant odors and is much easier to clean off.

Boilovers, Preventing

Simply adding a teaspoon of butter to the boiling water will stop the boilover in a few seconds.

Boils, Relieving Pain

Press some thin slices of brown laundry soap onto a soft piece of cloth, approximately three inches by three inches. Now, sprinkle about one teaspoon of white sugar onto the soap. Finally, put the poultice on the boil. Change it every twenty-four hours.

Bones, For Soup

They'll keep for a long time if you'll first place them in a hot oven (400°F) for ten minutes. When cold, wrap them in plastic to store them in the refrigerator.

Brass, Cleaning

If brass is blackened, make a paste of salt and pure lemon juice. Apply and scour with soft cloth, rubbing hard. When it is dry, rinse it with tepid water. Polish with a soft cloth or piece of flannel.

Or use orange Kool-Aid. It works. Make it as directed on the package/can. Apply the mixture with a cloth, rubbing hard. Then polish.

Bread, Baking

Place a small dish of cold water in the bottom of your oven, under the bread, to prevent it from getting too hard a crust.

Bread, Stale

Wrap dried out bread in a wet towel for thirty to forty seconds. Make sure it's completely covered. Then bake it in a slow oven (200°F) for thirty minutes. It will taste as good as new.

Bread Wrappers, Recycling

Plastic bread wrappers are excellent for wrapping food that you intend to freeze. They are also excellent and inexpensive cleaners for your gas or electric range. Simply crush them and rub them on the range to clean, polish, and prevent rust. Finish by polishing with a soft cloth.

Broiler, Smoking

Make sure your broiler is thoroughly clean, then put two or three cups of cold water in the bottom. As you broil, the water will absorb the grease and prevent the smoke.

Broken Glass, Picking Up

After all of the large pieces of broken glass have been picked up, use a slice of fresh bread to remove the slivers.

Or dampen a paper towel and gently rub it across the area.

Bronze, Cleaning

Dust well, then rub with a soft cloth soaked in linseed oil. Next, polish with a soft cloth.

Brooms, Preserving

When it's new, soak your broom for five minutes in hot, salty water, then leave it in the sunshine to dry. The salt toughens the fibers so the broom will last twice as long.

Or you can wash it in two quarts of warm water to which you have added one cup of household ammonia. Soak the broom in the mixture for one hour; rinse it in cold water. Then stand it on end in the sunshine. This will toughen it up considerably.

Brown Sugar, Keeping It Moist

When you put brown sugar into a container, add a piece of fresh, raw apple to keep it moist.

Or if it is an opened package, put it in the bread box with your bread for a couple of days. It will soften nicely.

You can also put the package in the refrigerator for twenty-four hours to keep it soft.

Bubble Gum, Removing

One of the easiest and most effective methods is to use lighter fluid, which removes it quickly, without stains.

Note: Be careful. Lighter fluid is very flammable.

Bulbs, Storing

Place them in an old nylon stocking and hang them in a cool, dry spot.

Bulbs, Watering

Never water bulbs from the top like normal indoor plants. If a bulb is in a small pot, stand it in an old soup plate with an inch of tepid water in the bottom. If the container is large, water the bulb by placing it in the bathtub in an inch or two of tepid water. Place it in an old towel to prevent scratching the tub.

Note: Never use very cold water on any plants. It will kill them quicker than anything.

Burns

If the skin is not broken, apply a soft cloth soaked in household ammonia. This method works wonders on minor burns.

You can also try one-quarter cup of linseed oil with the juice of one-half a lemon. Lightly rub the mixture over the affected area.

Or you can apply equal parts, or two tablespoons, of glycerine and the white of an egg. Rub it on gently, then bind the burn with a strip of soft cloth.

A small bottle of cold, strong tea kept near the stove is also a very good burn reliever.

Never put butter on a burn. Butter can actually irritate and contaminate a burn.

If it is a minor burn, run cold water over it, then apply a cold compress.

Burnt-On Food In Pots And Pans, Removing

Cover the burnt food with an inch of cold water, add two teaspoons of baking soda, and bring slowly to a boil. Then simmer for twelve to fifteen minutes. Discard the water and wash the pan in hot, sudsy water.

Butter, Clarifying

Let unsalted butter stand in a small container over a very low heat until melted. Gently pour off the butter, leaving the sediment in the bottom. Cool and use.

Butter, Softening

Fill a glass bowl, just big enough to cover the hard butter, with boiling water. After a minute, pour the water out and immediately cover the butter with the upside down bowl. Heat from the warmed bowl will soften it in a few minutes.

Butter, Stretching

Cut a pound of butter into small pieces and allow it to soften. Dissolve an envelope of unflavored gelatin in one-quarter cup of cold water and add this mixture to one and three-quarters cups of boiling fresh milk. Remove from heat and allow to cool. After beating the softened butter in a bowl, add the milk/gelatin mixture a little at a time, stirring constantly. Refrigerate it and it's ready for use.

Note: This is for table use only; not for cooking.

Buttons

If buttons keep coming off, use dental floss instead of thread. It is twice as strong.

Cabbage Odors, Preventing

If you are boiling cabbage, place a soup plate three-quarters filled with white vinegar on the stove, near the boiling cabbage, to absorb all the odor.

Cake, Keeping It Fresh

If cake is starting to get stale, put one-half of a freshly cut apple in the cake tin. It'll have it moist and fresh again within hours.

Cake, Keeping It Moist

One teaspoonful of glycerine added to each pound of flour will keep your cake moist.

Or you can add the grated rind of a lemon or an orange.

Cake Batter

Make sure that all ingredients, flour, butter, milk and eggs, are at room temperature. You'll get a much better cake with better texture.

Cake Flour, Substitution

Put two tablespoons of cornstarch in a measuring cup. Fill to the one cup measure with plain flour. Sift well and it's ready to use.

Cake Frosting

For an easy cake frosting, simply take one cup of powdered sugar and continue to add maple syrup until you achieve the desired consistency.

To spread cake frosting evenly, dip your knife blade (silver, if possible) in hot water and away you go. As the knife gets cold, redip it from time to time.

Cakes, Sticking To Pan

Before adding the batter to the pan, sprinkle the pan with equal parts of confectioners' sugar and flour.

Or, after baking, place the pan on an old beach towel that you've soaked in cold water then wrung out. After a few seconds, the cake will come out easily.

Candles

Any candle will burn twice as long if it is very cold. Put your candles in the freezer for two hours before lighting them. Or store them in the refrigerator overnight so they'll drip less as well.

Candles, Too Large For The Holder

Dip the end (about three inches) of the candle in hot water until it becomes soft and pliable. Now, press it down into the holder.

Candle Wax On Carpet Or Rug, Removing

First, remove as much as possible with a blunt instrument, for example, the back of a knife, and combing the spot with an old comb. Now, lay two paper towels on the spot and press with a warm iron. If a slight stain remains, rub it with a soft cloth dampened with alcohol. This will help remove stains caused by colored wax.

Candle Wax on Furniture, Removing

Apply a piece of soft cloth in which you have wrapped two ice cubes. When the wax becomes hard, scratch it off with the back of a knife. Apply wax and polish.

Note: Be sure to wipe up the ice water as it drips.

Candle Wax On Material, Removing

First, scrape off all excess wax. Next, put a paper towel under the wax spot, then lay another paper towel on top of the wax. With a fairly warm iron, press the paper towel for about two minutes. The heat melts the wax, which is absorbed by the two towels.

Candlesticks, Cleaning

Using a nail brush or other small brush, scrub them with sour milk. Then wash them in warm, sudsy water. Rinse in cold water, then polish.

Clean brass candlesticks with a nail brush that has been dipped in a thin mixture of pure lemon juice and household salt. Then wash, rinse, and polish.

Cane Furniture, Cleaning

Dust it well first, then scrub it with warm, salty water to which one-half a cup of pure lemon juice has been added. Dry thoroughly, then leave out in the sunshine.

Car, Stuck In Sand Or Loose Gravel

To get the needed traction, let the four tires down about one-third of the way. The extra width should allow your car to move much better.

Car Care

At least once a week, run your car at high speed (55 mph) for about five minutes, regardless of what speed you normally drive. This prevents carbon buildup in your engine, and later, costly repairs.

If your windshield wipers are leaving marks on the glass because of oil of grease residue, clean them by wiping the rubber section with a cloth soaked in white vinegar and sprinkled with baking soda.

To keep your water pump properly lubricated, add one ounce of brake fluid to your radiator twice a year.

Car Doors, Chipped

If the edges of your car doors are chipped from banging other cars, poles, and trees, clean as much of the rust off the edges as possible using steel wool dipped in kerosene. After it's dry, paint the edges of the car door with clear nail polish. Two or three coats applied with a cotton swab will work wonders.

Car Radiator, Cleaning

If the radiator is badly rusted, dissolve one cup of sal soda in one gallon of warm water and put it in the radiator. Run the engine for fifteen minutes. Then drain and rinse thoroughly two or three times.

Car Wash

For an easy way to wash your car, simply mix equal parts of warm water (no soap or detergent) and kerosene. No hosing down, before or after, is necessary. After washing, as the kerosene starts to bead, polish with a soft white cloth.

Cards, Stuck Together

If your playing cards are sticky and hard to handle, sprinkle them with talcum powder, then shuffle them a few times.

Carpet, Cleaning

Use very lightly moistened bran. Sift it evenly over the area, then vacuum or sweep in the usual way.

Note: Be careful not to moisten the bran too much.

Carpet, Fading

To restore the color, sprinkle the area liberally with household salt. Work it into the carpet or rug with the fingertips or a broom. Leave it for three to four hours, then vacuum very well.

Carpet, Flattened

The best thing to do is to wet the area with cold water just before retiring at night. The moisture causes the carpet to "stand up" during the night.

If this fails, next morning hold a steam iron three inches above the carpet and steam for three to five minutes. While steaming, brush the pile up and down and finish by brushing the pile up. Let it dry.

Carpet, Freshening

Make a mixture of one gallon of cold water and one and one-half cups of salt. Apply with the end of a broom after shaking out as much water as possible. This will brighten the carpet and keep the dust down.

Or you can use wet tea leaves. This method also works wonders.

Carpet, Removing Grease

Immediately cover the affected area with flour, whiting, or cornstarch. Leave for two hours, brush off the flour, whiting, or cornstarch; then rub the spot with a cloth soaked in turpentine.

Carpet, Removing Muddy Spots

Sprinkle common salt on the affected area. Wait ten to fifteen minutes, then sweep up the salt with a small brush.

If the carpet remains moist, dry it with paper towels pressed down with some heavy object, or use your hairdryer.

Carpet, Stained With Soot, Lead, Or Black Shoe Polish

A soft cloth soaked in rubbing alcohol should do the trick.

A teaspoon or two of fuller's earth with one-half cup of cold water and one-half cup of ammonia is also very good. Apply to the affected area and rub from outside to center, both clockwise and counterclockwise. Allow the area to dry, then brush well.

Carpet, Vacuuming

Always run the vacuum cleaner or brush across or with the nap. Running it against the nap forces the dust into the carpet.

Carpet Hole, Repairing

If the hole is not too large, clean up the edges of the hole, or if it is burnt, scrape off all the burnt edges. Now, pluck some matching fibers out of the carpet. Squeeze some quick-drying glue into the hole and, using tweezers, insert the fibers into the hole. When the glue is dry, gently brush the nap upwards.

Carpet Sweeper, Improving Its Efficiency

To improve your carpet sweeper's effectiveness, first comb the brushes while the sweeper is upside down and remove as much lint, hair, and dirt as possible. Now, with the fingertips, moisten the brushes. You'll find it improves the pick-up tremendously.

Carrots, Cooking

A lot more flavor is retained if they are cut lengthwise, whether baking them or boiling them.

Cats, Itching And Scratching
See Dogs, Itching And Scratching

Cauliflower, Boiling

Adding two tablespoons of pure lemon juice or vinegar to the water will improve the taste and keep it snowy-white.

Or add one-half cup of fresh milk to the water. This method also works wonders.

Celery, Keeping It Crisp

Lay it in a dish of cold water, then slice a raw potato into the water. Let it stand for three hours, then remove the celery from the water. It'll be as good as new.

Cereal, Soggy

Heat a heavy iron skillet over medium heat. Remove from the heat and pour cereal into the skillet. Cover tightly and leave for thirty minutes. Cereal will be crisp and crunchy again.

Cheese

Any cheese retains its flavor, even when hard as a rock. Save it and grate for spaghetti and soups.

Or grate it and grind it, then mix with grated, raw onion for a spread.

Cheese will grate much easier if chilled first.

To prevent cheese from hardening, wrap it in a soft cloth soaked in white vinegar. Wrap it completely, then put in a cool, dry place. Note: Only use the refrigerator as a last resort.

Cheesecake, Easy Cutting

Use a twenty-four inch length of dental floss. Works smoothly.

Chestnuts, Baking

First, soak them in clean, cold water for one hour. Remove and cut crossed in each end of the chestnut. Bake them in a 350°F oven until the shells curl up, usually about twenty minutes. If they still haven't curled, give them another fifteen minutes. Cool them and the shells are easily removed.

Chestnuts, Freezing

First, peel off the hull, or outside shell, then boil the chestnuts for fifteen minutes. Lift out of boiling water, cool, then remove husk, or skin of the nut. Put back in boiling water and boil for another fifteen minutes. Remove from water, cool, then place the chestnuts, sliced or whole, in a plastic freezer bag and season with one teaspoon each of salt and sugar. Shake, seal, and place in the freezer. They will keep for twelve months.

Chewing Gum, Removing

Put two or three ice cubes in a soft cloth, then place directly onto the material. Wait ten minutes, then break off the frozen gum.

Note: If the gum is stuck on a thick carpet, use an old comb to clean the area.

Chicken, Boiling

Rub the chicken or chicken pieces thoroughly with pure lemon juice to improve the flavor and retain the color.

Chicken Coating, Making Your Own

Mix together: four cups of plain flour, four cups of unsalted cracker crumbs, two teaspoons of salt, two tablespoons of white sugar, two teaspoons of onion salt, two teaspoons of garlic salt, three tablespoons of paprika, and one-quarter cup of salad oil. Mix together, then transfer to a brown paper bag if you are using it immediately, or an airtight jar to store in the refrigerator for later use.

Chicken, Tenderizing

Rub the inside and outside of the chicken with pure lemon juice about fifteen to twenty minutes before baking or frying and it'll be tender and tasty.

Chilblains, Healing

Ordinary household salt, slightly dampened, is as good a cure as any. Rub the salt into the affected area.

Note: This method is only for unbroken chilblains.

Chilblains, Preventing

Before leaving the home, rub turpentine well into the feet. Repeat the process when you arrive home. Done properly, it usually works wonders.

Chimneys, Cleaning

To help clean your chimney, put a piece of zinc on the hot coals.

Or throw a handful of salt on the wood from time to time to cut the smoke in half.

Chimney Soot

Chimney soot is an excellent fertilizer, so don't throw it away. Scatter it in your garden soil or mix it with your indoor plant soil.

China Dishes, Broken, Repairing

If no instant glue is available, the next best thing is two tablespoons of alum, melted. Apply directly to each side of the broken piece using a cotton swab. Press the pieces together and then hold them firmly for one minute.

China Dishes, Repairing Cracks

Put the cracked dish in one quart of cold fresh milk to which you've added three tablespoons of white sugar, then bring slowly to a boil. Continue to slowly boil for one hour. Allow the china to cool in the milk. Most small cracks will disappear.

China Dishes Or Ornaments, Preventing Cracks

Never plunge a hot piece into cold water or vice versa. The sudden change of temperature will crack them very easily.

Chives, Preserving

Fresh chives will keep for weeks if you wrap the green end of the chives in wax paper and keep them in the refrigerator.

Chrome, Cleaning

Moisten a soft cloth with kerosene and rub briskly. Polish with a second piece of soft cloth.

Cigarette Smoke And Cigar Smoke, Getting Rid Of

Before guests arrive, put a bowl of white vinegar in each corner of the room.

Or use a saucer full of fine charcoal to absorb a lot of the odors.

After the guests have departed, soak a large beach towel in cold water, wring out most of the water, then fan the smoke-filled area.

Clams, Opening

If they're the hard-shelled variety, simply pour boiling water over them. If it doesn't work the first time, repeat the process.

Closet, Musty

If the closet is musty, remove all articles, vacuum thoroughly, then wipe down all areas with a soft cloth dipped in one cup of ammonia, one-half cup of white vinegar, and one-quarter cup of baking soda in one gallon of fairly hot water.

One or two charcoal briquettes placed in various spots will keep closets free from musty odors.

Coat Hangers, Preventing Slippage

Your trousers won't slip off if you put one leg over the crossbar, then place the other leg the opposite way. This balances them nicely.

Coconut Matting, Cleaning

Make a mixture of warm, soapy water and give it a good wash and scrub. Rinse thoroughly with cold, salty water. Shake well, outdoors if possible, and hang it out in the sunshine.

Coffee

If percolated coffee tastes bitter, next time add a pinch of dry mustard to the water to restore the real coffee taste. For better tasting coffee, put the ground coffee beans in a heat-proof container or a piece of heavy-duty aluminum foil made into a saucer shape and put it in a preheated 325°F oven for about three minutes. It works wonders.

Note: This does not work for instant coffee.

Coffee, Cocoa, And Tea Stains, Removing

If the stains are fresh, rub a few drops of glycerine into the material, rub gently, then wash in warm, sudsy water.

Note: If the stain is old, soak the item in glycerine, preferably in a soup plate if the stain is not too large, for at least two hours, then wash in cold water and strong detergent.

Coffee and Tea Stains In Cups, Removing

Wet the cup with cold water, then sprinkle baking soda into and/or around the cup. With the fingertips, give it a good scour. Wash and rinse.

Coffee And Tea Stains On Materials, Removing

If it is a fresh stain, let very hot water run through the material from about six to nine inches. From time to time, remove from under the water and rub the spot hard.

Coffee Percolator, Cleaning

Put two tablespoons of baking powder in the percolator and let it boil for three to five minutes. Rinse thoroughly two or three times with clean, cold water.

Note: Don't put the pieces back together until it has dried completely.

Cold Remedy

Nothing will cure the common cold, but fresh chicken soup is considered one of the best cold relievers. Sipped hot at bedtime, it does unstuff the nose and chest.

Cold Remedy, Making Your Own

Mix together two tablespoons of finely powdered resin, four tablespoons of white sugar, and the whites of two eggs in one quart of good American whiskey. Take a tablespoon three times a day, preferably just before a meal.

Note: This remedy is also good for a weak back or an irritating cough.

Collars, Shiny

Most of the shine will disappear if the collar is saturated with white vinegar, then pressed from the reverse side while still moist.

This also works for shiny shirts, trousers, and coats.

Colored Materials

To prevent color from fading or running, add one teaspoonful of Epsom salts to each gallon of water, both washing and rinsing water.

Note: If black material is fading, try soaking it in ammonia after washing. Rinse by hand, don't use the dryer, and let the fabric dry in the open air, keeping it out of direct sunshine.

Cookies

After washing and thoroughly drying the cookie jar, put a crumpled piece of tissue paper in the bottom of the jar to soak up any moisture.

Note: Change the paper once a month.

A slice of bread or a quarter of a fresh apple in the cookie jar will soften cookies and prevent them from becoming hard and brittle.

Cooling Rack, Substitution

Invert a muffin pan to make a marvelous emergency cooling rack in the kitchen.

Copper, Cleaning And Polishing

Make a paste of one cup of any kind of flour, one cup of salt, and warm white vinegar. Apply and rub well with a soft white cloth, let dry, then wash in warm, soapy water. Rinse well and polish.

Or cut a fresh lemon in half. Dip the flesh of the half-lemon in salt, then rub onto the copper. After it dries, wash in hot soapy water, then dry and polish.

Corduroy, Cleaning

Hold a steam iron over the material, not touching it, and steam for twenty to thirty seconds. When the fabric is damp, use a small nail brush and vigorously brush the nap in both directions. Always brush the nap up to finish.

Corks

If a cork is too large for a bottle, soak it in very hot water for about five minutes so it will go in easily.

Corn, Keeping It Fresh

Stand the corn ears, stem down, in about one inch of cold, clean water. They'll be fresh and moist when you cook them that night.

Corn-On-the-Cob

For the best flavor, boil it with the husks still on.

Cotton Stockings, Recycling

Old cotton stockings, cut down the seam, make excellent dusting cloths.

Cranberries, Cooking

Add one-quarter teaspoon of baking soda to the cranberries while they're cooking and you'll use less sugar, as well as bring out the real cranberry taste.

Cranberries will keep for months if kept covered in a bucket of cold, clean water.

Crayon On Clothing, Removing

Scrape off as much as possible with the back of a knife. Soak in very hot water, as long as it's safe for the material, to which you've added three-quarters cup of baking soda. After five minutes, sprinkle the area with detergent and scrub between the fingers. After this, wash in the usual way.

Note: If the washing machine causes the stains, take the items to the dry cleaners.

Crazy Glue, Removing

The best thing to use is a soft cloth soaked in fingernail polish remover.

Cream, Preventing Curdling

Adding a pinch of bicarbonate of soda before mixing or beating will prevent cream and milk from curdling or souring.

Cream, Whipping

Add the white of an egg, then chill the cream for twenty minutes and it'll whip easily.

Or add a few drops of pure lemon juice or a sprinkling of plain gelatin powder to the cream.

Creaming Butter And Sugar

Before creaming butter and sugar, soak the bowl in very hot water for three minutes and the task will go twice as fast.

Note: Be sure to dry the bowl before starting.

Crepe de Chine, Keeping the Gloss

To preserve the gloss, add one tablespoon of powdered sugar to your wash water.

Crickets, Getting Rid Of

Place some fresh cucumber peelings around the room, on the sink, under the refrigerator. Crickets don't like its smell.

Or crush up a dozen moth balls, mix them with one cup of dry boric acid, and sprinkle it around your rooms, especially in the corners and in dark spots.

Still another method is to mix two cups of powdered borax, one cup of boric acid, and one teaspoon of any red pepper. Mix dry, then place in affected areas. One teaspoon of the powder in each corner of the room is a good start. You can also sprinkle it along the floor and wall joinings, and under the sink and refrigerator.

Cucumber

Before peeling, simply run the edge of a fork along the skin, pressing the prongs in about one-half inch, to give your cucumber slices a lovely serrate look.

Currants, Raisins, And Fruit, Baking With

Always coat them with flour to prevent them from sinking to the bottom and always add them to the mixture at the last minute.

Curtains

Slip a thimble over the end of the curtain rod and the curtain will slip through easily.

Or cut the finger off an old cloth glove and pull it over the end of the curtain rod.

Note: Don't use leather gloves. They prevent slippage.

Curtains, Removing Smoky Smell

To remove a smoky smell from curtains, simply soak for at least two hours in cold water to which powdered borax has been added. Then wash in the usual way.

Cut Glass, Cleaning

Dip a nail brush in warm water (no soap). Shake the brush out, then dip in baking soda. It'll come up sparkling.

Cutting Board, Removing Odors

Wet the board, then give it a good scrub with salt. After scouring, let it dry, then wash and rinse it well in clear, hot water. Allow it to dry in the open air.

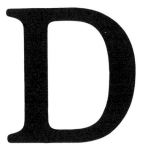

Damp Larder, Garage, Cellar

Place an old soup plate, or something similar, filled with lime in each corner of the room, or in the larder, on the bottom shelf. It will absorb any moisture.

Note: If dampness persists, change the lime every thirty days.

Dandruff

To keep it under control, use mouthwash. After the normal shampooing and rinsing, pour mouthwash directly onto the scalp and let it dry.

Or rub salt into the dry hair, then massage for five minutes before washing your hair.

Dandruff Remover, Making Your Own

Dissolve a dozen aspirin tablets (any brand) in one-half cup of warm water. Apply to scalp and gently massage for fifteen minutes. Rinse out thoroughly in lukewarm water.

Decals, Removing

Soak a cloth in warm white vinegar and place it on the decal. Repeat two or three times, and then scrape off the soaked decal with the back of a knife.

Dents In Wood, Removing

If dents are not too deep, the best thing is to place a cloth (cotton is best) soaked in warm white vinegar directly over the dent. Leave it there for one hour, keeping the cloth wet with more warm vinegar as it dries out. Then, after an hour, press the moist cloth with a fairly warm iron for about three to five minutes. The dent should disappear.

Note: Repeat if necessary.

Deodorant Stains, Removing

Soak the affected area in warm white vinegar for twenty minutes. From time to time, work the material between the fingers in the vinegar. Now, wash in the normal way.

If the stain remains, soak in denatured alcohol or sponge it with a cotton ball for ten minutes. Wash in warm, sudsy water.

Diamond Rings, Cleaning

Soak them for twenty minutes in white vinegar, then rinse and polish.

Dogs, Itching and Scratching

To stop the itching and scratching, sprinkle the dog or cat with powdered brewer's yeast and rub it in with the ends of your fingers. Even if they lick it off, it won't hurt them; brewer's yeast is good for them.

Or mix three tablespoons of olive oil with one tablespoon of sulphur and rub it onto the area of itching. This is also a good healer.

Dogs, Keeping Them Off Your Property

Buy one-half ounce of oil of cloves at the drugstore, then mix it with one gallon of warm water. Fill a spray bottle and spray your grass, steps, and sidewalk. One spray a week is usually enough to keep them away.

Dogs and cats also hate hot pepper. Run a hot pepper through your blender, add an equal amount of warm water plus a teaspoon of liquid detergent. Strain and spray it onto the area using a spray bottle if possible.

Dog And Cat Hairs On Upholstery

Soak a sponge in warm white vinegar and squeeze out most of it, then brush the sponge lightly over the upholstery. This method works on plastic, cloth, or leather upholstery.

Dog And Cat Rinse

The best rinse is one-half cup of dry or fresh rosemary in one quart of water. Boil, remove from heat, and let it cool. Strain it if using fresh rosemary. When it's cold, pour it, a cupful at a time, over the dog or cat. If possible, let them dry in the sunshine so toweling won't be necessary.

Dog And Cat Stains On Carpet Or Rugs

If the stains are fresh, soak up as much as possible with paper towels. Next, sponge the area with equal parts of white vinegar and cold water. Repeat two or three times, blotting well after each application.

Note: After the final application, the carpet or rug can be dried with an electric hair dryer.

Dog Food For A Picky Dog

At mealtime, mix one can of meaty dog food (your choice) with two teaspoons of apple sauce and one teaspoon of cottage cheese. This recipe never fails.

Doggie Cookies, Making Your Own

Mix together six tablespoons of wheat germ, three tablespoons of dry powdered milk, and one small jar of creamed chicken baby food. After mixing thoroughly, shape into small balls, then flatten on an ungreased cookie sheet. Bake in a 350°F oven for fifteen minutes. Your dog will love them.

Door, Squeaking

If your door is squeaking, it's almost certainly the hinges. A light spray with any vegetable oil spray, followed by a few swings back and forth, should stop it immediately.

Or rub any kind of soap on the door hinges. Make sure it penetrates the hinge, then swing the door back and forth a few times.

Double Boiler Cooking

One-half teaspoon salt added to the water in the bottom of a double boiler will bring it to a boil much quicker.

Drain, Clogged

Pour one cup of salt, followed by one cup of baking soda, down the drain. Now, boil one gallon of water or one-half gallon of white vinegar and pour it down the drain. If possible, seal the top of the drain and wait thirty minutes. Use the drains normally after this; it should be cleared.

Drawer, Sticky, Hard To Slide

Remove the drawer, then rub either candle wax or soap on the bottom and side runners of the drawer, as well as inside the piece of furniture.

Drawer Knobs, Loose

Remove the loose knob from the drawer, then paint the screw section with nail polish. Reinsert the knob and it's as good as new.

Dumplings

Buy a can of uncooked biscuits. Remove them from the can and allow them to rise at room temperature. Now, cut each biscuit in half and drop into your stew, casserole, or gravy. Cook uncovered for ten minutes, then lower the heat and cook covered for another ten minutes.

Dry Or Rough Skin
See Skin, Dry Or Rough

Dusting Cloth, Making Your Own

Get a piece of flannel about two feet by two feet and soak it in liquid paraffin for three hours. Afterwards, wash it in warm, sudsy water, then let it dry in the sun. It will be extremely good for dusting and can be used for months, despite repeated washings.

Or dip a two foot by two foot piece of cheesecloth in one-half pint of hot water to which you've added one-quarter cup of lemon oil. Hang it in the sun to dry.

Earthenware, Preventing Cracks

Whether it's a brand new teapot, a pie dish, or
basin you can prevent cracks by placing the
earthenware in a pot of cold water before using it
the first time. Bring it slowly to a boil. Boil for
three minutes, then remove from heat and let it
cool.

Earthworms In Potted Plants, Removing

Add one-quarter teaspoon of carbolic acid to a
pint of tepid water. Pour it over the plant soil,
about one-quarter cup to each pot.

Eggs, Beating

They beat a lot easier and make a much better
cake if left out at room temperature for two to
three hours.

Eggs, Boiling

An egg should never be boiled in vigorously
boiling water. It actually ruins the taste. The best
results are obtained by simmering the water. It
takes only a little longer, but it pays off.

Eggs, Brown Or White

Apart from the color, there is absolutely no difference between brown and white eggs. Buy whichever is cheapest.

Eggs, Cracked

A cracked egg can be boiled normally if you add one-half teaspoonful of vinegar to the water.

Eggs, Cracked, Boiling

If an egg is cracked, add two or three tablespoons of white vinegar to the water before boiling the egg. The vinegar will seal the crack.

Or wrap it in wax paper, twisting both ends tightly, then boil the egg in the wax paper.

Eggs, Good Or Bad

Gently put each egg into a glass of water. If it sinks it's good, but it if floats, it's a "baddie."

Eggs, Hard Boiled, Removing Shell

As soon as the egg is boiled, put it in very cold water. Leave it for two minutes, then remove the shell easily.

A simple method of crushing the shell is to roll the egg on a hard surface under your hand, applying medium pressure.

Eggs, Poaching

A little vinegar added to the water prevents the egg from running and spreading and keeps the yolk from breaking.

Eggs, Preserving

Never wash an egg. It removes the protective film. To make them keep longer, lightly coat each egg with vaseline before storing them.

Eggs, Preventing Cracking

Add two teaspoons of salt to the water to stop the shell from cracking.

Or, using a pin, prick a small hole in one end.

Eggs, Separating

Break the egg into a small plastic funnel. The white will run through, while the yolk remains.

Egg Yolks, Leftover

Drop into boiling, salted water in a frying pan, and they'll cook evenly. This way they're great on a sandwich, or you can break them up into a salad.

Egg Yolks, Preserving

Put them in a container (a cup is perfect for two or three) and cover them with cold water. Leave them in the refrigerator and spoon them out as needed.

Egg Stains, Removing

If the fabric is washable, soak it in cold water for five minutes, then wash in the usual way.

Note: If the fabric is unwashable, use rubbing alcohol. Do not use hot water; it sets the egg stain.

Egg Whites, Beating

Never beat egg whites in an aluminum pan. They will darken it.

Egg Whites, Whipping

To get egg whites to whip easily, put the egg in cold water for five minutes before separating it, then add a pinch of salt to the white.

Or, while beating the egg whites, add a pinch of salt to the bowl.

Eggplant, Removing The "Bite"

Slice the eggplant, then soak in very salty cold water for forty-five minutes. Rinse thoroughly, and it's ready.

Electric Light Bulbs, Energy Tip

Always keep your electric light bulbs clean. Dust them at least twice a month. Dust, grime, and insects can reduce the efficiency by as much as fifty percent.

One 100 watt bulb gives fifty percent more light than four 25 watt bulbs, yet uses the same amount of electricity.

Unless for a special purpose, never use colored bulbs. They give only half the light.

Embroidery, Pressing

Never press an iron directly onto the material. Always press embroidery from the reverse side.

Enamelware, Removing Food Stains

Use water with one tablespoon of baking soda or one-half cup of white vinegar added. Boil for five minutes, then rinse thoroughly.

Enamelware, Strengthening

When new, put it in a large pot, cover with cold water, then bring it slowly to a boil over low heat. Remove from heat and let the water cool. This will give it twice the normal life.

Enamelware, White, Removing Stains

Put the stained enamelware in a pot of equal parts of white vinegar and cold water. Add a tablespoon of baking soda, then, over medium heat, bring to a boil. Boil hard for five minutes, then allow to cool They'll be as white as snow.

Envelopes

If the glue fails to work, try a few drops of any nail polish. It sets like cement.

Epoxy Glue, Removing

Soak a soft white cloth in lacquer thinner. Place it on the glue for thirty seconds to soften it, then wipe it off.

Evaporated Milk, Whipping

Scald it first for about ten minutes in the top of a double boiler, then chill thoroughly. It whips very easily when it's very, very cold.

Eyeglasses, Cleaning And Polishing

A few drops of white vinegar will clean and polish them as good as anything.

Eyeglass Cleaner, Making Your Own

A tablespoon of cold water and a tablespoon of ammonia mixed in a small medicine bottle is very handy for polishing your glasses.

Fabric Softener Sheets, Making Your Own

Simply sprinkle a dry face cloth with three to four tablespoons of any liquid fabric softener. Toss the face cloth in the dryer with your clothes.

Fabric Softener Sheets, Recycling

Don't throw them away. They can be used three or four times in the dryer, then used as interfacing for cuffs, collars, dresses, and other items. It saves you money.

Face Freshener

In hot weather, squeeze some fresh lemon juice, strain it, then freeze it in an ice-cube tray. Rub the frozen ice cube over the face and it feels wonderful.

Note: Lemon juice cubes are also marvelous in icy cold water as a summer drink.

Facial Mask For Oily Skin

Mix together two tablespoons of wheat germ powder and two tablespoons of plain yogurt. Rub onto the face, massage well with fingertips, then let dry for fifteen to twenty minutes. Rinse off with clean, cool water.

Fat, Clarifying

Heat the fat over medium heat, then add two peeled, sliced potatoes, depending on the amount of fat you have. Allow the potato slices to fry until brown. Remove the potato slices, then strain the fat through a piece of cheesecloth into a clean container.

Fat In Soups And Casseroles, Removing

A large lettuce leaf dragged across the mixture will pick up most of the fat. Repeat with another lettuce leaf if necessary.

Or put two to three ice cubes in a piece of cheesecloth and drag it across the mixture. You'd be surprised how much grease will stick to the cloth.

Fat Or Oil, Splattering

One of the easiest things to do is to simply sift or sprinkle a little flour into the hot fat or oil. It works immediately.

Feet, Hot, Burning, And Tired

In a large dish, dissolve three tablespoons of Epsom salts in hot water to which you've added one cup of white vinegar. Soak the feet for at least twenty minutes, keeping the water as hot as possible by adding more hot water from time to time.

Note: The hotter the water, the better. Now, dry the feet thoroughly, sprinkle with boric acid or talcum powder and, if possible, raise your feet for five to ten minutes.

Or dissolve one tablespoon of alum in hot water and soak the feet for twenty minutes (following the procedure above).

Ferns

Cold, leftover tea is a very good tonic for them. To help them grow, use it to water them once a week. You'll see the difference.

If your ferns are turning yellow, slice two small raw potatoes in half and put the four halves (white sides down) on top of the soil. The potato draws out the worms which are usually responsible for the yellowing.

A weak solution of ammonia, one tablespoon to each quart of tepid water, is a marvelous vitalizer for ferns.

If the ferns are infested with worms, stick the heads of ordinary matches into the soil, about one inch deep. Use three to four for small ferns, five to seven for large ones. The sulfur in the matches gets rid of them.

Fever Blisters Or Cold Sores

Put two teaspoons of alum in a small, eight-ounce bottle and then fill with warm water. Shake vigorously to dissolve the alum, then apply directly to the blister. Keep repeating, if possible, every thirty minutes.

Or apply turpentine directly onto the blister or sore, using the fingertip. It is a very good healer.

Fire In Your Broiler

Quickly closing the oven door and turning off the heat should extinguish the flames in a few seconds.

Fire Starter, Making Your Own

Don't throw away any of your milk cartons. Cut them into strips, about six inches by three inches. They are excellent kindlers.

Fireplace, Removing The Sooty Smell

Crumble up about six or eight sheets of newspaper and lightly sprinkle some ground coffee beans over them. Light the papers and allow them to burn to ashes.

A few coffee grains thrown onto an open fire will remove the burning wood smell.

Fish, Frying

Never fry fish in lard or butter. Lard smells and butter fries a bad color. The best thing to fry in is a good salad oil.

Always cover the pan while frying to keep the steam in and cook the fish quicker. It will be tastier, too.

Fish, Salted

To draw out the salt, soak the fish in equal parts vinegar and cold water.

Fish, Thawing

Thaw frozen fish in a dish of cold fresh milk. It'll give it a fresh-caught flavor.

As an added treat, soak the fish in pure white vinegar for five minutes after thawing it in fresh milk. You'll be amazed at the improved taste.

Fish Odors On Cooking Utensils

Wash utensils in hot, sudsy water to which you've added three tablespoons of ammonia.

Fish Odors On Hands, Removing

Wash your hands in hot, salty water for one minute to remove the fishy smell. Never use soap until all the hot, salty water has been rinsed off.

Fleas In The House, Getting Rid Of

Fleas don't like rock salt. Sprinkle it very lightly around the affected rooms, particularly under the lounge, behind the television set, in a closet. You might also try putting a small amount in a soup plate in each corner of the room.

Or mix together two cups of powdered borax with one cup of crushed moth balls. Sprinkle it into your carpet or rug and work it in with your fingertips. Leave it there for at least six hours or overnight. Then vacuum thoroughly.

Note: The mixture can also be sprinkled under the cushions of your lounge, love seat, chair.

Fleas On Dogs, Preventing

Buy some 50 milligram vitamin B1 tablets or some brewer's yeast tablets or powder. Give a large dog two tablets a day; a medium-sized dog, one tablet a day; a small dog, one-half a tablet a day. If using brewer's yeast powder, use tablespoons and mix it with the dog's food.

Or mix equal parts of oil of thyme or eucalyptus oil with olive oil. Put a few drops here and there on the dog's skin and gently rub it in.

Another method is to sprinkle brewer's yeast (powdered) onto the dog and rub it in with the fingers.

In the dog's kennel, under the sleeping cloth, place some black walnut twigs with leaves. It helps drive the fleas away.

Sprinkling cedar wood chips under the dog's sleeping blanket is another good deterrent.

Flies, Getting Rid Of

If they're small black flies, they're probably breeding in the soil of your indoor plants. Get rid of them by making a mixture of warm, soapy water, then pour on one-half to one cup of the liquid, depending on the size of the plant, once a week.

Note: Any bar soap can be used, although naphtha soap works best.

If they're white flies (snow-white variety), mix together one tablespoon of liquid detergent in one gallon of tepid water. Spray under the leaves of your indoor plants. To kill the larvae as well, repeat the spraying every four or five days for two weeks.

Oil of sassafras is also very good for getting rid of flies. A few drops here and there work wonders.

Or mix together one-half teaspoon of white pepper, one teaspoon of brown sugar, and one tablespoon of thick cream. Set is out in a saucer. Believe it or not, it works.

Floors, Varnished

Never wash varnished floors with hot water. A cloth wrung out in lukewarm water is best. Each piece of the floor must be washed and dried immediately.

Flowers, Keeping Them Fresh

First, pull off all leaves that are going to be underwater. Now, mix together the following: two tablespoons of white vinegar and two tablespoons of cane sugar in one quart of tepid water. Arrange your fresh flowers loosely in the vase, and they'll keep fresh twice as long.

Or mix one teaspoon of salt to each quart of clear cool water. Two tablespoons of loose charcoal, fish tank variety, in the bottom of the vase is also recommended.

Drop a couple of aspirin in the water. It actually is good for fresh flowers.

Foot Warmer, Making Your Own

Put three or four cups of salt in a skillet and, over low heat, warm it up. When hot, pour into a large, thick sock and tie it with a string. It holds the heat for hours and can be used as a foot or hand warmer both indoors and outdoors.

Frames, Gold Leaf, Cleaning
See Furniture And Frames, Gold Leaf, Cleaning

Frankfurters, Cooking

Boil just enough water to cover the required number of frankfurters. After the water boils, remove from heat, add the frankfurters, cover tightly, and let stand for about eight minutes.

French Fries

To retain their crispness and bring out the flavor, soak them in cold, clear water for thirty to forty minutes before frying.

After drying them with paper towels lightly sprinkle them with flour. They'll fry to a golden brown.

Fresh Bread, Hot, Cutting

The best way is to put the bread knife blade in very hot water for two to three minutes.

Fresh Flowers

Never stand them on a television set or near a stove or oven. The heat from either will kill them very quickly. A cool, well lighted spot is best.

Also, if cutting them yourself, always cut the stems in a long slant, never straight across. It'll double their life.

Fresh cut flowers love fresh air. Airing the room daily is great for them. However, keep them out of drafts.

Frost On Windshield, Preventing

Purchase a heavy but supple, not stiff, sheet of plastic about twelve feet long. Put one end inside the door on the driver's side, then close the door. Pull it across the windshield, holding it in place with the wipers, then open the door on the passenger side. Put the other end inside and close the door.

Note: This works very well and is also very handy in snowy or icy weather.

Or put a full-sized newspaper on the windshield at night, securing it with the wipers. It must be a whole newspaper, not one or two sheets.

Frosting

Unless specifically instructed in the recipe, never frost a warm or hot cake. A cold cake is much easier to apply frosting to.

Frozen Pipes, Thawing

Use your hair dryer to thaw frozen pipes. Hold it about two or three inches away from the pipe and let it run hot. This works, usually, in a few minutes.

Fruit Stains, Removing

If still moist, cover the affected area with dry, powdered starch, Rub it in, let it dry, and rinse in cold water, then wash in the usual way.

If it is a dry stain, apply a paste of powdered borax and cold water. Rub in well, then let very hot to boiling water run through the material from the reverse side.

Or, if the stain is dry, dampen a block of camphor and rub it into the stain. Wash in the usual way. The stain will disappear. This method is good for clothing or tablecloths.

Furniture, Removing White Rings

Warm camphorated oil is best for removing white rings on furniture. Put the bottle in hot water for a few minutes, put a few drops on a soft cloth and apply.

Or moisten a cloth with kerosene.

Note: If the wood is dark, iodine may be used in place of camphorated oil.

You can also try putting a dab of any toothpaste on a soft cloth. Buff well. If it is a really stubborn ring, add a sprinkling of baking soda to the toothpaste.

Or try cigar or cigarette ash, moistened with glycerine. Rub lightly, then, when dry, polish with wax.

Furniture, Renovating

Rub it with a soft cloth moistened with linseed oil or paraffin. Rub it in well, then polish with a soft cloth or chamois.

Furniture, Repairing Cracks

Beeswax is excellent for filling such cracks. Apply it to the affected spot, then polish well with a piece of silk.

Furniture And Frames, Gold Leaf, Cleaning

Mix together one cup of denatured alcohol with two cups of cold water. Apply with a soft cloth that has been soaked in the mixture, then dry immediately.

Furniture Odors, Preventing

Buy about two pounds of red cedar shavings (furniture manufacturers of mills have them). Put a pound each in two old nylon stockings and place them in two bottom drawers. If the furniture has no drawers, lay the cedar shavings in the bottom.

Furniture Polish, Making Your Own

Mix one cup of sweet oil (odorless olive oil) with one-half cup of turpentine. Apply with a soft cloth, then polish briskly.

Or mix together equal parts of linseed oil, white vinegar, and turpentine. Apply with soft cloth, rub briskly, then polish with a second soft cloth.

Furniture Scratches, Removing

First, if the scratch is not too deep, try any cream wax or furniture polish. If this doesn't work try linseed oil, a matching colored crayon, or a melted candle. Polish well.

Or try iodine, applied with a cotton swab, if it's dark furniture. Melted shoe polish in a matching color is another solution.

Or rub the scratch with the meat of a Brazil nut.

Furs, Cleaning

If the fur is white, rub equal parts of salt and flour into it. Wait twenty minutes, then shake the fur vigorously and finish it with a good combing and brushing.

Or rub in cornmeal, then shake, comb, and brush.

To clean, as well as deodorize, fur, lay it in a large soft cloth that has been soaked in alcohol. Rub French chalk well into the fur. Roll up the fur in the cloth and leave for two days. Remove the cloth and give the fur a very good combing and brushing.

Garbage Bags And Cans

Put some pure ammonia into a spray bottle and give your bags and cans a good spray just before putting them out into the street. Dogs will give them a wide berth.

Gas Tank, Energy Tip

A full gas tank gives much better performance than a partially filled one. Keeping it full prevents condensation and prevents water getting into your gas tank.

Gasoline Stains, Removing

Quite often a disfiguring ring is left when gasoline dries on delicate materials. This can be prevented by adding one-half teaspoonful of salt to warm, soapy water before applying it.

Note: Gasoline is very flammable and every precaution should be taken when using it. Always use it outdoors, if possible, and keep it clear of heat or flame.

Gilt, Cleaning

Pat the area lightly with one-half a freshly cut lemon. Don't press too hard. Next, dab the area with lukewarm water to which you've added a little bicarbonate of soda. Use one pint of water to one-half teaspoon of bicarbonate of soda.

Gilt Frames, Cleaning

Never rub a gilt frame. The best method is to pat the area with a soft cloth, moistened with equal parts of ammonia and denatured alcohol. Follow immediately with another soft cloth and pat it dry. Now, move on to next area.

Note: A few drops of lemon oil, patted on twice a year with a soft cloth, will prevent the gilt from cracking.

Glass Cooking Utensils, Removing Stains

Fill the utensil with fairly hot water, then dissolve baking soda in the water. Use one tablespoon of baking soda to each quart of water. Let it stand until cool. Wash in the normal way.

Glass Decanters, Cleaning

Pour one-half cup of white vinegar into the decanter, then carefully add two tablespoons of raw rice. Shake well, wait five minutes, then shake hard again. Remove the rice and vinegar, then wash in warm, sudsy water. Now rinse with cold water.

Glass Jar Tops, Removing

A simple method which often works when a jar top is hard to remove is to stand the jar upside down in enough very hot water to cover the jar. Wait three to five minutes, then dry the top and start turning.

Sometimes a few sharp taps with the back of a knife will do the trick. Remember, turn left to loosen, right to tighten.

Glasses, Cleaning

One teaspoon of household ammonia added to the rinse water will make your glasses sparkle. Let them air dry, then polish.

Glasses, Preventing Cracks

If you want to pour very hot liquid into a glass, always put a metal spoon in the glass first. A dessertspoon is best. Then pour the hot liquid onto the spoon.

Glasses, Stuck Together

Stand the bottom glass in hot water, then pour cold water into the top glass. The glasses should come apart in twenty to thirty seconds.

Glassware, Delicate, Washing

Even very hot water will not crack it if you slowly slip it into the water. Never plunge glassware into hot water.

Glassware, Strengthening

Simply put the glassware in a large pot of cold, salted water. Over low heat, let the water come to a boil. Remove from heat and let the water go cold. Gives the glassware double strength.

Glue, Removing

Whether fresh or dried, the best thing to remove glue is hot, but not boiled, white vinegar. If old and hard, press a hot cloth on the glue a few times to soften it.

Glue, Thinning

If glue is thickened in the bottle, add a few drops of warm white vinegar and give it a good stir. After a few drops it should return to normal.

Note: Don't add too much vinegar, only a few drops at a time.

Gold, Cleaning

Most hot, barbecue sauces have been found very useful in cleaning gold.

Also soak in pure household ammonia for five minutes. Then wipe and polish.

Grandfather Clock, Cleaning

Soak a pad of cotton wool with turpentine and place it in the bottom of the clock. The rising fumes help to clean the insides of the clock and oil the mechanism.

Grass, Growing In Cement Sidewalk

Simply pour boiling, salty water directly onto the grass.

Note: To keep it away, spoon in common, dry salt from time to time.

Grass Seeds, Protecting

Before scattering them on your lawn, soak them in bluing and cold water until they are thoroughly colored. The birds won't eat them (they don't like blue), and it doesn't affect the fertility of the grass seeds.

Grass Stains, Removing

If the stain is fresh, hold the affected area under the cold water tap and work it between the fingers as the water runs through. This method should remove it all within a few minutes.

Note: If the material is not washable, the best thing to use is rubbing alcohol, rubbed in well.

Or rub molasses into the stain, work between the fingers, then wash in the normal way.

Karo syrup, worked into the old stain, is another good grass stain remover. When the stains break up, wash in mild, sudsy water, then rinse thoroughly.

Grease And Oil On Cement, Removing

Add one cup of washing soda to one gallon of very hot water. When dissolved, apply to the cement with a stiff scrubbing brush. Keep repeating until oil or grease disappears. Rinse thoroughly with cold, clean water.

Note: Be careful; washing soda will burn the skin.

Grease, Axle Grease, Removing

Rub the area with lard, work in well, then soak the material in turpentine. Sponge with clean turpentine and continue rubbing until dry.

Note: Turpentine is flammable, so don't use it near a stove, oven or open flame.

Grease On Silk, Removing

Lay the material flat on a clean, white cloth. Cover the spot with powdered French chalk. Lay a sheet of blotting paper or two paper towels over the chalk and press with a fairly warm iron.

Note: If it doesn't get all the grease on the first attempt, repeat the process.

Grease On Suede, Removing

The best method is to use glycerine applied with a soft white cloth. Keep rubbing. Spots will disappear within a few minutes.

Grease On Varnished Wallpaper

Wash it with a soft cloth dipped in a mixture of one pint of warm, sudsy water to which two tablespoons of ammonia have been added.

Grease On Wallpaper

Make a paste of alcohol and French chalk. Apply to the spot and leave it overnight. Next morning, when the alcohol has dried, brush the spot lightly. Repeat if necessary.

Or put a paper towel or blotting paper on the grease spot and press with a fairly warm iron.

The heat through the blotting paper or paper towel will absorb the grease.

Grease Spots On Material, Removing

Quite often, grease spots can be removed with hot, sudsy water. Try this method before anything else.

Also, you can scrape off as much as possible with a blunt instrument. The back of a knife works well. Then rub lard into the spot. Rub well into the grease spot, then repeat the scrape-off method. Now, launder in the usual way.

Green Peppers, Stuffed

After stuffing them, place them one at a time in a greased muffin pan. It prevents them from bursting and helps them retain their shape.

Green Vegetables, Preserving The Color

Add a pinch of baking soda to the water and keep the cover off the saucepan.

Hair, Removing Static Electricity

If you can't get your hair to sit down long enough to spray it, take a fabric softener sheet and rub it on your hair. It works like a charm.

Hair Conditioner, Substitution

Apply one-half cup of mayonnaise to your dry, unwashed hair. Massage well with the ends of the fingers for five minutes, then cover your hair with a large plastic bag for fifteen to twenty minutes. The bag can be held to the head with a rubber band. Shampoo your hair in the usual way.

Hair Shampoo, Making Your Own

Mix four ounces of soft soap from the drugstore with twelve ounces of distilled water. Bring slowly to a boil, then remove from heat and let it cool. As it cools, stir in a few drops of your favorite perfume or aftershave.

Hairbrushes, Cleaning

First, comb out all the old hair in the brush. Then wash thoroughly in equal parts of cold water and ammonia. Shake well, then let dry in sunshine.

Note: If it is an ebony brush, coat the ebony with Vaseline before putting it in the ammonia. Rub it off later.

Ham, Boiling

Prevent the ham odor by boiling it in water to which you've added one-half cup of vinegar.

Ham, Too Salty

To remove as much salt as possible, place the ham in a large, deep baking dish, then pour two bottles of beer over it. Cover it tightly with foil and/or a lid and slowly bake in a 400°F oven for two hours. No basting is necessary.

Handbags, Black Leather, Cleaning

Dust first, then rub with a soft cloth that has been dipped in a mixture of two teaspoonsful of fresh milk and one teaspoonful of sweet oil (odorless olive oil). Rub well, allow to dry, then polish with another cloth which has been sprinkled with any good furniture polish.

Handbags, White Or Beige, Cleaning

Follow the same procedure as above, except polish with a cloth sprinkled with white shoe cream.

Handkerchiefs And Towels, Bleaching

Soak overnight in a gallon of cold water to which you've added one tablespoon of cream of tartar.

Hand Lotion

Stand a bottle of pure glycerine in fairly hot water until it's lovely and warm. Applied every night before retiring, it's the best lotion in the world.

Hands, Dirty, Stained, Cleaning

For sweet smelling hands, add a tablespoon of white sugar to your warm, soapy water. They'll smell like a rose.

Hard Water

If soap fails to lather, add one-quarter teaspoon of olive oil to the water. It helps tremendously and will prevent rough skin.

Hard-Boiled Eggs, Slicing

You'll have no crumbling when slicing hard-boiled eggs if you dip your cutting blade in cold water or fresh milk.

Hats, Cleaning

If you are cleaning a felt hat, particularly a white or light colored hat, one of the best things is a thick slice of stale bread. Cut off the crust and rub with the white portion.

Health Drink

Old-timers claim that two tablespoons of apple cider vinegar mixed with two tablespoons of honey is a marvelous drink, good for colds, coughs, stomach, and eyes. Try it twice a day for ten days.

Hearth Tiles, Cleaning

If tiles are not badly stained, instead of scrubbing them use a good furniture or floor polish. They'll really shine.

Heat Rash, Relieving

Apply dry, double thick cornstarch to the rash. This will bring relief in a few minutes.

Heating, Energy Tips

If possible, close off any room that you're not using, such as laundry, kitchen (after the meal at night), spare bedroom. You'll be surprised at how much fuel you'll save.

If a draft is coming into the room under the door, press an old beach towel against the bottom of the door.

Also pull down the window shades at night, as well as closing all your drapes. It does make a difference.

Hiccups

Place a teaspoonful of white sugar in your mouth and when it has dissolved let it slowly trickle down your throat.

Or press your pulse fairly hard for seven seconds, then release.

Honey, Preventing Granulation

Keep it in the dark.

If it turns sugary, stand the jar in hot water, stirring occasionally until the granulation is gone.

Horseradish Sauce, Making Your Own

Wash the horseradish thoroughly. Run it through a grinder or blender to grate it very fine. Then combine each cup of horseradish with one-half cup of white vinegar. Seal tightly in clean jars and store in the refrigerator.

Hot Pad, Substitution

Simply invert a muffin pan near your oven or stove, and you'll save yourself hours of cleaning.

Hot Water Bottles, Preserving

Fill the bottle three-quarters full with flat soda water, then shake it vigorously for two minutes. Dry thoroughly, then wrap completely in blue tissue paper or black and white newspaper.

Household Odors, Removing

Visit the drugstore and purchase a small bottle of oil of wintergreen. Tie a piece of thread to a cotton ball, for easy handing, and put a few drops of oil of wintergreen on it, then hang it at various locations in your residence.

Caution: Don't accept synthetic oil of wintergreen. Keep trying until you get the real oil.

I

Ice Cream Stains, Removing

If the stains are fresh, hold the material under the cold water faucet and, as the water runs through, work it between the fingers.

If it is an old stain, soak it in cold white vinegar for twenty minutes, then wash in warm, soapy water. Rinse well and allow to dry in the sunshine.

FIRST TAKE DRUGS.

Ice Cubes

Hot water freezes faster than cold water in your freezer.

If the guests are coming, empty your ice cube trays early, then put the cubes into a plastic container in the refrigerator. You'll have plenty of ice to start and more on the way.

To prevent your ice cube trays from sticking in the freezer. spray the outside with a vegetable oil or lightly coat them with grease.

Ice On Sidewalk Or Steps

The best thing to use is rock salt from the hardware store, but ordinary household salt can be used in an emergency.

Note: A bag of rock salt in the trunk of the car is handy in icy conditions. A few handfuls under the wheels will give extra traction on icy driveways and roads.

Indoor Plants, Preventing Bugs

When you plant a seedling, plant a clove of garlic along with it. As the plant grows, so will the garlic. Cut the garlic down from time to time and there will be no smell and no bugs.

Indoor Plants, Restoring The Gloss

If the plant has hard leafed foliage, the best thing to use is glycerine. Put a few drops in a piece of soft cloth and rub it onto the leaves.

If the leaves are soft, soak a cloth in equal parts of fresh milk and tepid water.

Indoor Plants, Sickly

Use the water you boiled your eggs in to pep up sickly indoor plants. It's full of minerals and does help them.

Or make two holes in the soil with the end of your finger. Into each hole pour a teaspoonful of Geritol. Don't laugh; it works.

Cold tea leaves are an excellent fertilizer for all indoor plants.

Ink, Ball-point, Removing

If the stain is fresh, give it a good spray with hair spray. Allow it to dry, then brush it off with a small brush or wipe it off with a cloth dampened with white vinegar.

Or soak it overnight, or not less than four hours, in fresh milk or buttermilk, then wash in warm, sudsy water, rinse well, and dry in the sunshine.

Or you can rub lard into the affected area. Let it stand for twelve hours, then wash in the usual way.

Another method is to soak it for eight hours minimum in sour milk. After this, wash the item and rinse well.

If the stain is fresh, pour denatured alcohol through the material. Then work it between the fingers and wash it in warm, sudsy water.

Ink On Carpet, Removing

To remove blue ink, but not ball-point ink, apply salt to the area immediately. As the salt becomes stained, brush it off with a small brush and tray. Keep adding salt until it is no longer stained. After the final brushing, finish by rubbing the area with a soft white cloth moistened with warm white vinegar.

Or, if the stain is dry, soak it in fresh milk or buttermilk for three to five hours or overnight if you can. Next morning, wash it in warm, sudsy water, rinse well, then dry it in the sunshine.

Ink On Leather Or Plastic, Removing

Moisten a soft cloth with rubbing alcohol. A few minutes of gentle rubbing will remove all traces.

Ink On Paper, Removing

The best thing to use is fresh milk, applied carefully with a cotton swab.

Note: Repeat the process if necessary.

Ink Stains, On Fingers And Hands, Removing

Dip a nail brush in warm white vinegar, shake it, then dip the brush in salt. The stains should disappear very quickly after a few scrubbings.

Insomnia

A small raw onion, eaten fifteen to twenty minutes before retiring, is often the answer. It does work in many cases.

A glass of warm milk with a teaspoon of brandy added is another proven method.

Or turn the mattress over and around. It often makes the difference.

Iodine Stains On Linen, Removing

Rub the stained area with a slice of fresh lemon. If it doesn't work the first time, repeat the process. Wash in the usual way.

Or you can try making a paste of dry mustard and a few drops of cold water. Apply and let stand for four hours. Brush off the mustard.

Iron, Cleaning

If the bottom of the iron is stained, sprinkle salt on a sheet of wax paper, then slide the lukewarm iron back and forth across the salted wax paper. Polish with a soft cloth, plus a few drops of a good silver polish.

Or while the iron is hot, rub a candle onto the base. Now, rub it off and polish it with a thick, clean cloth.

Or you can spray the iron with oven cleaner. Wait one minute, then wipe and polish. The small holes can be cleaned with a toothbrush.

Note: Do not use oven cleaner on teflon-coated sole plates.

Iron, Cleaning The Interior

Fill the cold steam iron with equal parts of white vinegar and water or pure white vinegar if it is very dirty. Steam over the sink for about five minutes. Let it stand for thirty minutes, then rinse it thoroughly with clean, cold water two or three times.

Ironing

Always iron standing on a thick carpet or rug. You won't tire so easily and your legs won't ache.

Sort out the clothing as you iron. This will save you a lot of time.

Make an easy-to-use sprinkling bottle by punching one or two small holes in the screw-top of an old ketchup bottle.

Also, always use warm water when dampening clothes. It's more easily absorbed and makes clothes easier to iron.

Remove the ironing board cover, then place heavy duty aluminum foil over the ironing board. Replace the cover. The heat is reflected up and makes ironing so much easier.

Let the iron do the work. A hot iron is a lot easier to use than a warm one.

You can easily dampen delicate things by rolling them up in a damp beach towel for about thirty minutes.

Iron Pots, Removing Dark Stains

Half fill the pot or skillet with cold water to which you've added a half cup of white vinegar and three tablespoons of salt. Boil for fifteen minutes. It works.

Itching Dogs, Curing

After bathing the dog in the normal way, dry the dog, then rub in pure tomato juice. Do not rewash.

Note: Do this every three days for two weeks and the itch will disappear.

Itching Skin, Caused By Grass, Dust, Seeds, Sun

Dip a bar of any laundry soap in cold water and rub it on the affected area. Let it dry. This should stop the itching in seconds.

Or rub the itch with cold white vinegar.

Applying dry, double thick cornstarch to the itch is also helpful.

Ivory, Cleaning

Wash it in warm sudsy water, rinse well and dry. Next, apply furniture cream to polish it.

Ivory, Stained, Yellowing

After cleaning, following the procedure above, apply pure lemon juice or bleach and leave it out in the sunshine.

Or apply cream silver polish on a soft cloth, rub hard, then polish with a second soft cloth.

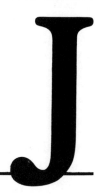

Jam Or Preserves

Always rub butter over the bottom of the pan before adding fruit. It prevents sticking and burning and keeps the jam clear.

To prevent your jam from going sugary, add a pinch of citric acid to it just before removing it from the heat.

If jam has gone sugary, stand the jar in hot water for ten minutes, stirring constantly. The sugar will dissolve and the jam will return to normal.

Japanese Beetles, Getting Rid Of

Open a medium sized can of fruit cocktail, then let it stand in the sun until it ferments, usually about a week. Put some bricks inside a large bucket or container and stand the can of fruit cocktail on top of the bricks. Next, fill the container with cold water until it reaches the top of the can.

Note: Light-colored containers (white, yellow, beige, or pink) are the best attractors.

Jeans, Rejuvenating

The next time you wash a new pair of jeans, add a couple of old pairs to the washing water. The dye and sizing from the new jeans will completely rejuvenate the older ones.

Jello

Instead of water, use the juice of canned or fresh fruit to make the jello taste better.

Jellyfish Stings

Take a bottle of meat tenderizer to the beach to rub directly on the skin if stung.

Rub plenty of baby oil onto the skin before entering the water to prevent stings.

Jewelry, Leaving Dark Marks On Skin

Clean the jewelry, dry and polish it thoroughly, then coat the inside of the jewelry with liquid nail polish.

Jewelry, Restoring The Shine

Put the jewelry in three cups of cold water with one cup of ammonia added. Bring to a boil over medium heat for five minutes. Immediately rinse under hot running water.

Note: You might also give the jewelry a light scrub with a toothbrush while under hot running water. This will remove any clinging residue. Wipe it well and polish with a soft cloth.

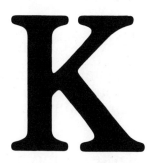

Kettles

Any type of kettle, particularly aluminum, will last twice as long if emptied at night, turned upside down and allowed to stand.

Note: The dishwasher rack is a good place to put it.

To remove lime deposits, fill the kettle with two parts of white vinegar and one part water, then boil for twelve to fifteen minutes. Allow to stand for five minutes, then empty the kettle and rinse it thoroughly two or three times.

Note: The water will reach boiling point twice as fast, so removing the sediment can save you money.

Kid Gloves, Cleaning

If the gloves are white or brown, pull them onto the hand, then rub them firmly with a soft cloth moistened with warm, sudsy water to which a little fresh milk has been added. When clean, hang them out to dry in the open air.

Note: Try to wet the gloves as little as possible.

If they are black kid gloves, pull the gloves on, then clean with a mixture of good quality blacking and olive oil. Rub in well, then hang in the open air.

Knives, Cleaning

A paste of baking soda and water with a teaspoonful of bicarbonate of soda added helps remove stubborn stains.

Knife, Removing Fish Odors

If a knife is used for cutting and/or scaling fresh fish, remove the odor by rubbing it with half a lemon.

Or cut a small fresh potato in half and rub the blade.

Knives, Storing

After washing and polishing knives, rub them with a little sweet oil on a cloth, then wrap them individually in flannel to prevent tarnishing.

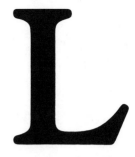

Lace

Never iron good lace. It'll dry flat and smooth if you wrap it around a clean glass bottle after washing it. Let it dry in the open air.

Lace, Torn, Repairing

Brush a little clear nail polish onto the edges of the tear, then carefully press them together. Once it has dried, washing will not hurt the nail polish.

Lace, Whitening

If lace is old and yellowing, soak it overnight in sour milk. Without washing or rinsing it, hang it out in the sunshine. When dry, wash in the usual way.

Lace Edging, Pressing

Always press from the material to the lace edging.

Lace On Dress, Cleaning

In most cases, lace does not have to be removed from the dress to be cleaned. Lay the lace flat, then rub in powdered starch. After at least four hours, brush off the starch.

Lamp Shades, Cleaning

After dusting with a soft cloth, wipe the shade with another soft cloth that has been lightly moistened with fresh milk.

If the shade is silk, dust it, then lightly rub it with a piece of cheesecloth sprinkled with any good dry soap powder. Then wipe and polish with another soft cloth.

If the shade is parchment or metallic paper, mix together one tablespoon of turpentine with half a cup of mineral oil. Apply the mixture lightly with a soft cloth, then gently wipe it off.

Leather, Preventing Cracking

One of the easiest things to apply is white Vaseline! Apply it evenly, then work the Vaseline into the cracks with the fingertips. Rub off any surplus.

Note: Follow this procedure for seven days and notice the difference.

Leather Furniture, Cleaning

Dust thoroughly, then wash with a good saddle soap. When it dries completely, polish with a reliable leather cream.

Leather Stains, Removing

The best thing to use is the white of an egg. Rub well into the stain, then, if possible, put the article out in the sunshine. Leave it for fifteen minutes, then rub off.

Leather Suitcase Or Trunk, Cleaning

Make a mixture of equal parts of boiled linseed oil and white vinegar. After dusting, apply the mixture with a piece of flannel or a soft cloth, then give it a good polish.

Note: Be sure to shake it well before using; oil and vinegar tend to separate. Don't boil the linseed oil, buy it. It's very flammable.

Leather Table Tops, Cleaning

Never use wax. First wipe the entire area with a soft cloth dampened with mineral oil. Keep rubbing until all wax buildup is gone. Now, apply lemon oil with a soft cloth. Rub in well. Reapply the lemon oil three or four times over the next two weeks.

Lemons

Soak lemons for five to ten minutes in boiled water that is still very hot. You'll get twice as much juice.

To keep lemons for a long time, rub the skin with paraffin and put them in a cool, dark place. When you are ready to use one, soak the lemon in boiling water for a few minutes and the paraffin will come off.

Or completely cover them with cold water and place them in a cool, dark place. Change the water every seven to ten days. They'll keep for months.

Lemon Extract, Making Your Own

Grate the rind of three large lemons into a half pint of grain alcohol. Let it stand covered for about five days at normal room temperature. After five days, strain the alcohol into a bottle, then add one ounce of pure oil of lemon. This method can also be used to make orange extract.

Lettuce, Separating Leaves Easily

After cutting out the stem, hold the lettuce under the cold water tap and let the water run into the stem hole.

Lettuce, Storing

Never store lettuce in plastic or cloth. It causes rust on the leaves. Storing it in a paper towel or paper bag keeps it fresh much longer.

Lid On Stainless Steel Pot, Removing

Simply put the pot back on the heat for a couple of minutes. The steel will expand and loosen the lid.

Linen, Storing

If storing white linen, always iron both sides, then wrap it in blue tissue paper.

Note: A good pressing will kill any moth eggs and the blue tissue paper prevents yellowing.

Linoleum, Cleaning

If you prefer not to wash it, dust it thoroughly, then moisten a soft cloth with paraffin and rub it over the linoleum to clean it like new and help preserve it as well.

An occasional rub with a soft cloth or piece of flannel soaked in olive oil is also good as a preservative for linoleum.

Any spots that have been dulled from constant use can often be restored by a good polishing with beeswax and flannel.

Note: Never scrub linoleum; it will scratch easily.

Linoleum, Keeping It In Place

Coat the bottom of the offending area with a good linoleum glue from any hardware store, then press it down. Hold it in place till dry with heavy books, bricks, or something similar.

Linoleum, Preventing Wax Buildup

Soak a cloth in gasoline and rub thoroughly.

Note: Open doors and windows and be certain not to smoke or strike a flame. Gasoline is very flammable.

Turpentine may be substituted for the gasoline.

Linoleum, Repairing Holes

Mix some grated cork with some liquid glue. Quickly apply to the hole, fill, then let it dry thoroughly. Add a thin coat of clear varnish and the linoleum will look new again.

Luggage, Cleaning

To clean and polish dull, grimy luggage, beat two egg whites till stiff, then, using a small soft cloth, rub well into the grain. As it dries, polish it with another soft cloth.

Marble, Cleaning

Dust thoroughly, then wash it with warm, soapy water. Stains can be removed with half a lemon dipped in whiting or baking soda. Wash it off immediately, then polish with furniture cream.

Note: Black marble should be polished with linseed oil. The older grain-type marble can be cleaned and polished with toothpaste.

Margarine, Stretching

Mix one pound of margarine in a bowl with three-fourths cup of salad oil and one cup of buttermilk. Beat well, then refrigerate for at least two hours.

Note: This is for table use only. Do not bake with it.

Material Fading, Restoring To White
See Whites, Fading

Mattress, Removing Stains

Whether wet or dry, rub the affected area with equal parts of warm water and white vinegar applied with a moistened, not soaked, cloth. Rub for two to three minutes, then dry up as much of the moisture as possible, using a soft dry cloth.

Note: A hairdryer is also very handy. When the mattress is dry, sprinkle it with talcum powder and rub in with the fingertips.

Note: If possible, put the mattress in direct sunshine for one hour.

Mayonnaise

When making your own mayonnaise, add the white of an egg to the mixture after the vinegar has been added to prevent curdling.

Or add half a teaspoon of pure lemon juice to the egg yolk before adding the oil.

Meat, Boiling

When boiling any meat (pork, chicken, beef), a pinch of baking soda added to the boiling water will make the meat tender.

Medicine Bottles, Cleaning

If the bottle is stained, put in a tablespoon of white vinegar, more if it's a big bottle, then add a teaspoonful of raw rice. Shake it vigorously for a few seconds, wait five minutes, shake hard again, then rinse in cold water.

Medicine Stains, Removing

Most medicine stains will come out if rubbed with alcohol.

Note: If it is an old stain, soak it in alcohol for twenty minutes, then wash in cold, soapy water.

Meringue, Preventing Shrinking

When you spread the meringue on your pie, make sure it touches every bit of the side. The crust will prevent it from shrinking.

Note: Never bake meringue in a hot oven. A moderate oven gives the best results.

Also, to make the best meringue, do not use cold eggs. Let the egg whites sit at room temperature for fifteen minutes before beating them.

Mice, Getting Rid Of

They hate the smell of camphor. Crush up a box of mothballs and sprinkle in your drawers, trunks, and cupboards.

If cheese isn't attracting mice to your mouse traps, try pumpkin seeds or a soft piece of bread smeared with peanut butter.

Mildew On Linen, Removing

Make a paste of two teaspoons of warm white vinegar, two teaspoons powdered detergent, and one teaspoon crushed white chalk. Rub well into the mildewed area, let it dry, then wash in the usual way. More detergent can be added if the paste is too moist! Rinse well, then dry in sunlight.

Or wet the mildewed spot with pure lemon juice, then sprinkle it with household salt. Rub the salt onto the area, then hang it out in the sun to dry. Brush off the salt with soft cloth after the item has dried.

Mildew On Tiles, Removing

Make a paste of one cup baking soda with enough bleach to make a thick paste. Apply it to the mildewed area, rub it in, then leave it for at least six hours. Rinse off with clear, cold water, dry, then wipe it with a soft cloth dampened with ammonia.

Milk And Cream, Preventing Souring

Add a pinch of bicarbonate of soda and give it a good shake.

Milk And Cream Stains, Removing

Never use hot water to remove milk or cream stains. Wash the material in cold water, then wash again in cold water and detergent. A final rinse in clear, cold water finishes the task.

Milk Pudding, Baking

Always place the pudding dish in a dish of water in the oven to prevent it from boiling over or burning.

Mincer Or Chopper, Cleaning

If your mincer or chopper is greasy after mincing fatty meat, remove most of the grease by mincing two slices of bread (not too fresh) through the machine. Now, wash it thoroughly in hot, sudsy water and rinse.

Mirror Cleaner, Making Your Own

Mix together two quarts of warm water, two tablespoons of kerosene and one teaspoon of powdered borax. Rub on with soft cloth moistened with the liquid.

Mirrors, Cleaning

Black and white newspaper is very good for cleaning mirrors. Soak the first piece of newspaper in cold water, squeeze it into a ball and clean, then polish with a second piece of newspaper, also squeezed into a ball.

Or make a paste of whiting and alcohol. Smear the mirror with the paste, using a cloth or gauze, then quickly rub the mixture off before the alcohol evaporated. Polish with a soft cloth.

Mirrors, Repairing Scratches

Make a paste of dry mustard with a little white vinegar. Apply the paste to the scratch with the end of your finger and gently rub until the scratch disappears.

Mites On Outdoor Plants

To get rid of mites, mix half a cup of buttermilk and four cups of wheat flour in four gallons of cold water. Spray it directly onto the leaves of your outdoor or ornamental plants.

Note: If your plants' leaves are turning yellow or twisting, mites are usually the cause.

Molasses, Syrup, Preventing Sticking

If you have to use these in a measuring cup, glass, or spoon, prevent sticking by wetting the inside of the utensil before using it.

Or lightly grease the cup, glass, or spoon with butter.

Moles, Getting Rid Of

Castor oil beans, dropped down the holes or scattered around the area, are an excellent deterrent.

Using carbide pellets or powder put in the holes and followed by boiling water, is also very effective. After pouring the water, cover the holes with bricks or wood. The gas is deadly to the moles.

Mosquito Bites

Soak a cotton ball in pure ammonia and apply to the bite to relieve pain and itch.

Or rub any yellow laundry soap directly onto the bite or itch.

Any good toothpaste rubbed directly onto the spot is also very good, and works in a few seconds.

Mosquito Repellent

Oil of citronella, available at the drugstore, can be rubbed on arms, neck, and ankles to repel mosquitoes.

Plain kerosene is another good deterrent.

Or use Liquid Smoke, rubbed lightly on the skin.

Outdoors, you might try throwing old rags or dry manure on an open fire. Mosquitoes do not like the smoke.

Moths, Getting Rid Of

Moth balls are still the best, of course, but here's another way. Insert six whole cloves in the top half of a fresh orange. It not only helps get rid of moths, but gives off a spicy odor as well.

Mustard Stain, Removing

Soak the spot with warm glycerine. Work the spot between the fingers for sixty seconds, then wash in warm, soapy water to which you've added two to three tablespoons of alcohol.

Musty Rooms, Freshening

Buy some new cedar chips at a furniture manufacturer or saw mill. Then place them in the leg of an old pair of panty hose. Tie off the end and place in the room. One or two of these will freshen your room for twelve months.

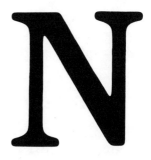

Nail Polish, Drying Quickly

After applying, give each nail a quick spray with any good cooking oil spray to make it dry quickly.

Nail Polish, Removing

The safest thing to use is denatured alcohol. Use a soft cloth to sponge the area with the alcohol. If the nail polish is dry, add a few drops of ammonia to the alcohol and continue to sponge until the nail polish breaks up. Wash with warm, soapy water.

If the material is not acetate, nail polish remover can be used. Use banana oil on acetate.

Nail Polish, Thinning

Stand the bottle in hot water, covering about half of it, for two to three minutes. It will become smooth.

If possible, keep the bottle in the refrigerator. You'll find it much easier to apply.

Nail Polish Remover

Why buy expensive nail polish remover? A small bottle of acetone from the drugstore is as good a remover as anything else.

Nails, Splitting The Wood

Before hammering, dip the point of the nail into melted paraffin wax. It'll prevent costly splits.

Or dip the point of the nail into a bar of any kind of soap.

Nails Or Screws, Inserting Into Plaster

First, to prevent the plaster from breaking or cracking, heat the point of the nail in very hot water before inserting or hammering.

To make it tight and prevent it from falling or working out, remove the nail or screw, fill the hole with fine steel wool and reinsert it. It'll stay tight for years.

To prevent plaster from shattering, put a strip of scotch tape over the spot. It's easy to remove after hammering the nail in.

Nickel, Cleaning And Polishing

Dampen a soft cloth with warm water, then rub it over soap or sprinkle it with soap powder. Bring to a good lather, then dip the cloth in salt and apply. When dry, polish with a soft cloth.

Nosebleed

Sit up, never lie down, and gently pinch together the soft part of the nose, about halfway up the nose. With the other hand, hold something very cold (an ice cube, a cold can of beer, a frozen article) on the back of the neck, just above the collar line.

Or, after pinching the nose for a minute, place ice cubes (one in each hand) on either side of your nose and hold till bleeding stops.

Oil, Purifying

Heat it in a pan on top of the stove, but don't boil it. Then drop in two slices of raw potato for five minutes.

Oil Fire

A good safety precaution is to have a brown shopping bag handy, filled with fine sand. If fire occurs, pour or throw the sand directly onto the fire. It will quickly extinguish it.

Note: The best place to keep the bag of sand is in the cupboard under the kitchen sink.

If sand is not available, salt or baking soda thrown on the fire will stop it. If the fire is in a pot, pan, or skillet, cover it with the lid as soon as possible.

Note: Never use water or a cloth to put out a fire. It could make it WORSE.

Oil Paintings, Cleaning

Remove it from the wall, lay it flat, then sprinkle salt onto the oil painting. Shake the painting from side to side for about five minutes. Next, turn the painting over and shake it until all salt is removed.

Onion Odors On Hands

Rub some dry mustard on your hands after peeling onions. Wait one minute, then wash hands in the usual way. You'll get rid of onion odors.

Or rub fresh lemon juice over the hands, let it dry, then wash off.

Onions, Peeling

Peel onions under water or pour boiling water over them before peeling them to avoid tearing while peeling them.

Orange, Peeling

Drop the orange in very hot water for five minutes to make the skin come off easily. The white membrane will pull off twice as easily, too.

Orange Extract, Making Your Own
See Lemon Extract, Making Your Own

Oranges And Lemons, Getting More Juice

If an orange or lemon is dried up, drop it into boiling water for five minutes. You will be surprised how much juice is in there.

Oysters, Frying

Before frying oysters, roll them in a mixture of two cups of dry cracker crumbs with one to two teaspoons of celery salt. It'll give them a magnificent flavor.

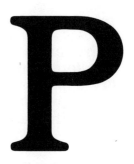

Paint Brush, Hardened

Soak a hardened paint brush in turpentine for two to three minutes. Squeezing the bristles between the fingers helps break up stubborn old paint as well. Rinse the brush thoroughly in fresh turpentine.

Or simmer the brush in hot white vinegar for twenty minutes. Then wash it in warm soapy water.

Paint Odor, Removing

Put a shallow baking dish in the center of a freshly painted room. Half fill it with cold water, then peel and cut a fairly large onion in half. Put the onion halves in the water, close the door, and leave it overnight. No odors will remain.

Paint On Floors, Removing

Whether it's wood, tile, or any other type of floor, the best thing to use is nail polish remover. Lay a dampened cloth flat on the paint stain for two or three minutes to soften the paint. Then wipe it off. Now, wipe the spot with a soft cloth soaked in warm, sudsy water, then polish.

Paint On Furniture, Removing

If the paint is fresh, use fine steel wool dipped in any liquid cleansing wax. If the paint is old or dry, apply a soft cloth soaked in linseed oil. Let the cloth rest on the stain for five minutes to soften the paint, then wipe it off.

Paint On Glass, Removing

A soft cloth soaked in hot, but not boiling, white vinegar will do the job. As it softens, scrape off the paint with a razor blade, then continue to rub.

Paint On Material, Removing

If the material is colored, dip the stain into turpentine for one minute, then work it between the fingers till the paint breaks up. Now, dip the material in ammonia for a few seconds, then wash by hand using warm water and detergent. Rinse well and hang out in the sunshine to dry.

Note: Do not wash in a washing machine or dry spin and be careful of flames when using turpentine.

Or if the paint is wet, and is on washable white material, wash it with hot water and detergent, then boil it in the same sudsy water, but add a teaspoonful of paraffin.

Note: If the paint is dry, soak in turpentine, then wash by hand and dry it in the sunshine.

Paint On Tiles, Removing

The best thing to use is a soft cloth soaked in turpentine.

Painted Walls, Cleaning

Mix together two tablespoons of powdered borax, one teaspoon of ammonia and two quarts of warm water. No soap is necessary. Apply this mixture with a soft cloth. It works very well.

Painting

Use fast drying glue to stick an ordinary paper plate to the bottom of the paint can. No more drips on floor or carpet.

Painting Doors Or Windows

First coat all locks, door handles, and hinges with a thin layer of Vaseline or petroleum jelly. After painting, it's very easy to wipe off and saves lots of work and worry.

Pancake Syrup, Making Your Own

Put one cup of granulated sugar, one cup of brown sugar and one cup of cold water in a small saucepan. Bring slowly to a boil, stirring occasionally. When all sugar is dissolved, add maple flavoring to suit your own taste.

Pancakes, Cooking

To prevent batter from sticking to the spoon, dip the spoon in fresh milk and it will drop off the spoon easily.

Paper Logs For Fires

First, roll up five or six old newspapers as tightly as possible. With wire, secure them with two or three bindings. Soak them thoroughly in very salty cold water. When they are completely soaked, about five minutes, remove them from the water and let the "logs" dry completely in the sunshine.

Paper Stuck On Wood

Using any sort of oil (cooking oil is very good), slowly soak the paper with a few drops at a time. Wait ten to fifteen minutes, then wipe off the paper and oil with a soft cloth moistened with white vinegar.

Parsley

Wash it in hot water and it is easier to chop and retains a lot more flavor, too.

Paste, Substitution

If no paste or regular adhesive of any kind is available, use the white of an egg.

Pastry

To keep pastry from sticking to your rolling pin, try rubbing flour on it before starting to roll the dough. If this doesn't work, place a piece of plastic on the pastry and roll through that. It works.

Add a few drops of pure lemon juice to your pastry mix to soften it up beautifully.

Patches On Clothing

After cutting out the patch to the required size, dip it in cold water. Flatten it out on the material, then sew it on. It won't have that wrinkled look when it is dry.

Patent Leather, Cleaning

Rub the patent leather with a soft piece of cloth lightly dampened with nail polish remover. Wipe it dry immediately. Apply a thin coating of Vaseline and polish briskly.

Peas, Cooking

If using fresh peas, boil the pods as well. It adds to the real pea flavor.

Peaches

After peeling peaches, dip them , whole or sliced, in fresh milk and no discoloring will occur.

Pecans, Removing The Shell

Cover pecans with boiling water and let them stand till cold, then gently tap or hammer the small end of the shell.

Perspiration Stains, Removing
See Deodorant Stains, Removing

Pewter, Cleaning

Apply a paste of whiting and linseed oil. Clean thoroughly, then wash in warm, soapy water. Rinse well, then polish with a soft cloth or chamois.

Or apply toothpaste to a damp soft cloth and rub. Buff well with a second soft cloth.

Piano Keys, Cleaning

If the keys are ivory, clean and polish them with a soft cloth moistened with alcohol.

Or wipe them with a soft cloth dampened with denatured alcohol.

Note: Never use soap on ivory. It yellows the keys.

If the keys are plastic, any type of toothpaste is a good cleanser. Simply rub it on, scour with the fingertips, then, as it dries, polish with a soft cloth.

Pickled Beets

They will keep twice as long and will not go soft if you add a pinch or two of dry mustard to the vinegar in the jar. Give it a little shake to mix it

Pickling And Preserving

Never use copper, brass, or zinc utensils in canning. Glass is best, but unchipped enamel is also good. Use whole spices if possible; ground spices may darken your preserves. Use non-iodized salt. It's the best by far. Store in a cool, dark place. For crisper pickles, put a green grape leaf in the bottom of the jar and another leaf in the top of the jar just before sealing.

Pie Crust

Pie dough is much easier to handle and makes a much better crust if all the ingredients are cool.

Place the lower crust in the pan flat and smooth, with no air under the crust.

Pie Crust, Soggy

Sprinkle powdered sugar on the crust before baking to avoid a soggy pie crust.

Or brush a well beaten egg yolk over the top crust to give it a lovely glaze.

If the bottom crust is soggy, next time brush the bottom crust with the white of an egg.

Pineapple, Growing Indoors

The top of a fresh pineapple, planted in a glass container with just enough tepid water to cover the bottom, about three fourths of a pint, will soon sprout and take root. Keep it in a warm, open area (near a window, perhaps) for best results.

Note: Gently twist the crown out; don't cut it out.

Pins, Keeping Them Sharp

Instead of laying them flat in a tin, stick them in a bar of toilet soap. It lubricates them, keeps them pointed, and makes them much easier to use.

Plastic Odors, Removing

Soak the item overnight in equal parts of cold water and white vinegar. This will keep them soft as well, whether they're tablecloths, curtains, or placemats. Rinse them well the next morning.

Plastic Shower Curtains, Cleaning

Put curtains into the washer with two large beach towels, then add half a cup of detergent and half a cup of baking soda. Fill the machine with warm water and run through the entire washing cycle. Add one cup of white vinegar to the final rinse water.

Note: Do not spin dry. If possible, hang them out in the open air.

Poison Ivy

Gently rub meat tenderizer directly onto the affected area to stop the burning.

Polishing Cloth, Making Your Own

Soak a white cloth in kerosene, then hang it out in the open air to dry. The cloth is very good for polishing varnished surfaces, chrome, venetian blinds, and glass.

Note: The cloth will last for weeks before needing another soaking.

Porcelain, Cleaning

One of the easiest methods is to sprinkle a piece of flannel with household salt, then rub. It usually works like a charm.

Porcelain, Removing Yellow Stains

Make a paste of crushed chalk, preferably white, and ammonia. Apply to the stain and scour with a stiff cloth or small brush. Allow to dry, then rinse off.

If porcelain on a pot or pan is burnt, try rubbing it with toothpaste. A good scouring with the fingertips usually removes most burnt spots.

Potatoes, Baking

To bake potatoes twice as fast, boil them in salted water for ten minutes before placing them in the oven.

Or soak them in cold, salted water for twenty minutes before baking.

Potatoes, Boiled

Add half a teaspoon of pure lemon juice to the water to keep peeled potatoes white and bring out the real potato taste.

If they're old potatoes, add one tablespoon of sugar to the water before boiling to improve the taste tremendously.

Potatoes, Keeping The Skins Soft

Rub the skins with olive oil or with the rind of a lemon before placing potatoes in the oven. Their skins will be soft and delicious.

Or wrap them individually in aluminum foil.

Rubbing the skins with bacon fat improves the taste as well.

Potatoes, Mashed

Add a well-beaten egg white to them to improve both the taste and appearance.

Potatoes, Preventing Darkening

Add one or two tablespoons of white vinegar to cold water. Cover tightly and raw peeled potatoes will keep for days in your refrigerator.

Note: Make sure the water and vinegar mixture completely covers the potatoes.

Pumpkin, Baking

Cut it to the preferred size, wash well, but don't peel. The outer skin helps retain all the flavor. When cooked, the skin is much easier to remove.

Putty, Substitution

Make a thick paste of linseed oil and whiting. It'll set hard, just like real putty, and is very effective.

Pajama Cord, Replacing

Fasten a medium-sized safety pin to one end of the new pajama cord. Work the pin between the fingers and the material will slip over the pin as you push it through.

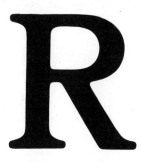

Rabbits, Getting Rid Of

Rabbits love strawberries, as well as the bark from fruit trees. Soak a pound of liver, cut up into two-inch pieces, in hot water for four to five minutes. Strain the mixture and put it in a spray bottle. Spray it on your brambles or fruit trunks. It discourages rabbits very quickly.

Talcum powder mixed with crushed mothballs is also a marvelous deterrent to rabbits. Sprinkle it liberally around your plants and vegetables and it repels them.

Note: Buy inexpensive talcum powder.

Rain Spots On Felt And Satin, Removing

Roll some white tissue paper into a ball and rub the affected areas in a circular motion. If the tissue paper becomes soiled, make another ball and continue to rub.

Razor Blades, Sharpening

If using a double edged blade, try this. With warm water, wet the inside of a glass, then, with two fingers, press the razor blade onto the inside of the glass and rub back and forth. Now, reverse the blade and repeat the process. You'll get many more shaves out of your old blade.

Red, Inflamed Eyes

Into one pint of water, pour one teaspoon of boric acid, then boil. When cool, apply to eyes with a dropper or eye washer. The solution works in five to ten minutes.

Refrigerator, Cleaning The Exterior

The best thing to use is one quart of warm water with one fourth cup of bicarbonate of soda. Then dry and polish it.

Note: A good polisher is ordinary wax paper.

Refrigerator, Energy Tip

Never put hot foods in your refrigerator. It takes a lot more power to cool. Let your food cool off first.

Refrigerator Odors

Two or three lumps of charcoal or one saucerful of fine charcoal will absorb odors and sweetens the refrigerator.

Or thoroughly wipe the inside of the refrigerator with a soft white cloth soaked in warm white vinegar.

Two tablespoons of vanilla essence in a small open bottle is also very good for odors.

Freshen your refrigerator by washing the interior every ten days with a solution of warm water and baking soda.

Restringing Beads

The next time you are restringing beads, instead of thread, use dental floss. It's twice as strong.

Rhubarb, Cooking

When cooking rhubarb, add two tablespoons of any red jello crystals to the water to take away the tartness. You'll use less sugar, too.

Or sprinkle a small amount of baking soda in the boiling water.

Ribbon

When washed, smoothly wrap it around a clean glass bottle and let it dry in the open air.

Rice

To each quart of water, add one teaspoon of pure lemon juice. It not only keeps the grains white, but also prevents them from sticking together.

Ringworm

One of the best cures for ringworm is vinegar or the brine from pickled onions. Rub it directly onto the affected area every sixty minutes.

Roaches, Getting Rid Of

Mix together one cup of powdered borax, one half cup of white sugar and one cup of flour. Add just enough cold water to make a "biscuit-like" mixture. Spoon it out, a teaspoonful at a time, then roll between the palms into small balls. Set them out to dry in the sunshine. When they are dry, scatter them around the affected areas, such as under the sink, in the laundry.

Note: If it is not a sunny day, dry them in a low oven (200°F) for ten to fifteen minutes.

Another solution is to scatter powdered borax in your cupboards, on floors, in the bathroom.

Roasting Beef

Always place the roast fatty side up. This way the drippings will automatically baste the beef.

Rose Bushes, Getting Rid Of Aphids

If new rose buds are covered with aphids, sprinkle black pepper on the buds. By the next day the aphids will be gone.

Rose Bushes, Getting Rid Of Pests

A few chives, planted beneath your rose bushes, will counteract pests and diseases.

Rubber Heel Marks, Removing

A soft cloth dampened with turpentine or kerosene is best. A good brisk rub usually erases them.

Rug Shampoo, Making Your Own

Dissolve one cup of soap powder in one gallon of tepid water, along with one fourth cup of clorox, one fourth cup of white vinegar and one fourth cup of dishwasher soap. Mix well, then put in your carpet shampoo machine.

Note: If no machine is available, apply with the ends of a stiff broom.

Rugs, Curling Up At Edges

Treat the curling edges with hot starch, applying it on the wrong side in about a four inch triangle. Then press the corner with a fairly hot iron.

Or buy some double faced tape, and apply it to each corner.

Rugs, Fading

Wash them in the bathtub in a mixture of warm water, two cups of white vinegar, and one cup of salt. Wash well, then allow them to dry in the sunshine.

Note: If rug is too large to wash in the bathtub, apply the same mixture with a piece of flannel while the rug is on the floor, then dry with paper towels or hairdryer.

Rugs, Slipping

With quick drying glue, stick a rubber ring (preserving jar rings are best) to each corner of the rug.

Rust On Car Doors
See Car Doors, Chipped

Rust On Ironware Or Furniture, Removing

The best thing to use is kerosene. Scrub the area with a nail brush dipped in the kerosene. After it dries, rub Vaseline into the holes to prevent further rusting.

Rust Stains On Material, Removing

Make a paste of equal parts of salt and cream of tartar moistened with white vinegar. Spread on thickly, work it in, then let it dry in the sunlight. Brush off the salt and cream of tartar with a soft cloth.

Or make a paste of pure lemon juice and salt. Work it well into the rust stain, then hang the clothing or material out in the sunshine.

Salad

To prevent salad from becoming soggy if it has to remain in the open for a long period at a barbecue, picnic, or party, place a saucer upside down in the bottom of the salad bowl before filling it with salad. It'll remain crisp and fresh.

Salad Bowls, Cleaning
See Wooden Dishes, Salad Bowls, Cleaning

Saltshaker, Keeping Salt Dry

Empty out the damp salt, wash the shaker, then dry it thoroughly. Fill the shaker three fourths full with fresh salt, but add eight to ten grains of raw rice. The salt will flow easily.

Saltshaker, Removing Rust

First, scrub it in hot, sudsy water, rinse well, then dry it thoroughly. Now, paint the inside of the metal top with clear nail polish. Let it dry completely.

Note: If the holes are painted over, prick them open from the inside with something sharp.

Sausages, Cooking

To prevent your sausages from bursting and shrinking, first boil them in the pan for about five to six minutes, Next, roll them in any kind of flour and fry them in the normal way.

Note: This method is good for any type of uncooked sausage.

Scent, Retaining The Fragrance

In hot, humid weather, the fragrance will quickly disappear. Next time, smear a thin coat of Vaseline or petroleum jelly onto the skin before applying the scent.

Scissors, Sharpening

Cut through some fine sandpaper for fifteen to twenty seconds.

Scorched Material

If the fabric is linen, plunge the garment into cold water immediately and leave it for twenty-four hours. Wash it in cold, sudsy water, rinse well, then hang it in the open air.

If it is a heavy scorch, cover the scorch with a soft cloth soaked with hydrogen peroxide. Cover with a dry cloth and give the material a good press with a hot iron. Rinse well after washing and hang it in the sunshine.

Or rub the scorched spot with half a raw onion. Work it in well, then wash in the usual way.

Self Rising Flour, Making Your Own

Put one and one half teaspoons of baking powder and one half teaspoon of salt into a measuring cup. Fill to the one cup measure with plain flour. Sift it well and it's ready.

Note: If more is needed, just double or triple the process.

"Setting" Colored Materials

If you want to "set" colors (pink to green), soak the material in a gallon of cold water to which two quarts of alum have been added. Now, wash in the usual way.

If you want to "set" dark colors (blues or blacks), soak the fabric in a strong, salty, cold water solution for twenty minutes. Now, wash in the usual way.

Sewing Machine, Oiling

After oiling with machine oil, sew through a piece of blotting paper for fifteen to twenty seconds. It'll absorb the surplus oil and prevent needless washing of your material.

Shaving Cream, Substitution

For one of the smoothest, cleanest shaves possible, use your wife's or girlfriend's cold cream.

Shine On Clothing, Removing

If the fabric is black crepe, faille, or gabardine, simply rub it with a piece of terry cloth towel dipped in white vinegar, then wrung out till merely damp.

Shoes, Damp

Add a little paraffin to the shoe polish and they'll shine up as good as new.

Shoes, Drying

Immediately stuff them with black and white newspaper. Make sure you don't overstuff them out of shape. Put them in a warm but airy place and let them dry.

Note: Never dry them in a stove or on a radiator. It'll make them hard as rocks.

Shoes, New And/Or Hard To Polish

Rub shoes with half a lemon. When the juice is dry, apply polish in usual way, then rub hard with a soft cloth or a piece of velvet.

Shoes, Squeaking

Use an icepick or something similar to make three or four holes about one half inch to three fourths inch apart in the soles, just behind the ball of the foot.

Or carefully insert a few drops of glycerine around the edge of the shoe where the sole joins the upper. Wipe off any residue.

Shoe Brushes, Cleaning

Wash shoe brushes in warm, soapy water to which you've added one half cup of turpentine. Be sure to wash the brush under water to save spraying your face with the mixture. Rinse thoroughly in a fresh sudsy solution with no turpentine. Shake well and let them dry in the sunshine.

Shoe Polish, Substitution

If you've run out of shoe polish, try your paste floor wax.

Or rub your shoes with wax paper.

Shortening, For Dark Cakes Only

Beat beef or mutton drippings till creamy, add one fourth teaspoon of lemon juice and a little bicarbonate of soda.

Silk, Keeping It Soft

A teaspoonful of salt, added to the washing water, will help keep the material soft and shiny.

Silks, Fading

Soak them for fifteen minutes in cold, sudsy water to which one half teaspoon of Epsom salts has been added.

Silk Stockings, Preserving

Always give them a final rinse in clear, cold water to which a little white vinegar has been added. It'll dissolve all remaining soap and give them a double life.

Silly Putty, Removing

The easiest and quickest thing to use is rubbing alcohol. Soak a cloth, lay it on the putty for fifteen to twenty seconds, then rub it off.

Silver, Cleaning

Completely line the kitchen sink with aluminum foil. Sprinkle three or four tablespoons of Spic-n-Span cleaner into the sink. Gently pour in boiling hot water. Add the silver and let it soak for ten minutes. Rinse in clean, tepid water and polish well.

Note: The silver must touch the aluminum during the soaking in order for the reaction to take place.

After polishing your silver, give it a good rub or spray with any good furniture polish to keep it shiny for months.

Silver, Preventing Oxidizing

Put six moth balls in the toe of an old nylon stocking. Put it in the cabinet with your silver, hidden perhaps in a vase, cup, or some other container.

In a jewel box, use a small piece of charcoal.

Silver, Preventing Tarnishing

After washing and polishing your silver, give your silver tray, mug and other items a thin coating of any clear hair spray.

If possible, stand it on a metal base covered with a thin cloth.

Silver, Removing Dark Spots On

Rub with half a potato dipped in baking soda. It removes dark spots quickly.

Or rub the dark spots with a dry cork. This method is quick and never scratches.

Or use tobacco ashes on a cloth dampened with vinegar.

Another method that works very well is to dampen a soft cloth and apply some toothpaste. Polish when dry.

Silver, Removing Egg Stains On

A pinch of salt rubbed on with the end of the finger will quickly remove the stain.

Silverfish, Getting Rid Of

Crushed moth balls are as good a deterrent as you'll get. Sprinkle them around the area where you know they are.

Or make a dry mixture of one half cup of boric acid, one cup of white sugar and one teaspoon of any hot pepper. Sprinkle it under the sink, wardrobe, crevices, and in all dark places.

Silverware, Storing

After washing and polishing silverware, wrap each piece in tissue paper. To be doubly sure, re-wrap in old newspaper and seal thoroughly.

Sink Smell, Getting Rid Of

Last thing at night, pour a cup of baking soda down the drain. The next morning, run some hot water for one to two minutes. The smell will disappear.

Pouring hot, salty water down the drain at least twice a week is also a good odor remover.

Skin, Dry Or Rough

Use the white of an egg. Just before retiring at night, rub it into the affected area. Wash it off next morning. Do this every night for fourteen days, and your skin will be soft and white.

Sweet oil (odorless olive oil) is also excellent for dry and rough skin, as well as facial lines like wrinkles and crows feet. Put the bottle of sweet oil in warm water for thirty seconds before applying. Wash it off the next morning.

Snails, Getting Rid Of

Sprinkle sawdust mixed with salt around the area. They hate the sawdust and the salt burns them. This mixture is good anywhere but particularly around young plants.

Or use stale beer. Empty the beer into a large shallow dish and place it in your garden to kill snails by the hundreds.

Note: This method is also good for slugs.

Scattering wood ash around your plants and flowers is another method. It is especially good for protecting the growth of young tomatoes, lettuce and peppers.

Note: Scatter the ashes liberally in the area; snails hate crawling over dry ashes.

Soap Pads

Cut soap pads into quarters. They'll still do the job and, over the course of a year, you'll save a lot of money. Why waste them?

Soap Saver

Save all small pieces of soap. When you have quite a few pieces, tie them into a piece of flannel and dip it in boiling water. After a few minutes, the soap pieces will soften to a jelly. Plunge them into very cold water and, as it cools down, form a ball with the soap pieces still inside the flannel. Let it firm completely, remove the flannel covering, and you have inexpensive soap.

Soft Drink Stains, Removing

If the stains are fresh (moist), place the material under the cold water tap and let the water run through. Work the material between the fingers till stains disappear. Wash in cold, soapy water.

Note: Never use hot water; it sets the stains.

If the stain is an old, dry stain, soak the affected area in equal parts of cold water and alcohol for twenty minutes. Now wash in cold, sudsy water.

Soup, Cooking

"Soup boiled is soup SPOILED!" It should be simmered gently and evenly.

Soup, Flavoring

If making vegetable soup, add one fourth teaspoon of nutmeg to enrich the flavor, or add half a fresh apple, chopped, to give the vegetable soup a delicious flavor.

Soup, Greasy

Skim the surface with a large lettuce leaf, or put two ice cubes in a piece of cheesecloth and drag it across the soup.

Soup, Keeping

Never let it cool in a covered pot, and never keep it in a warm area or it will quickly sour. Pour it into the desired container, let it cool, then cover and keep in a cool place.

Soup, Thin

Add a little grated cheddar cheese. It will improve the flavor immensely.

Soup, Too Salty

Add a teaspoonful of sugar or a few small pieces of raw turnip.

Or grate a raw potato into the soup.

Soup Seasoning

Always add seasonings very gradually so you won't over-flavor.

Sore Throat

Gargle a mixture of the following: One half teaspoon of salt and one half teaspoon of powdered borax in three fourth of a tumblerful of warm water. When the salt and borax are dissolved, gargle.

Note: Do not swallow the solution.

Or mix together two tablespoons of white sugar and two teaspoons of sulfur. Every four hours, take one teaspoonful, letting it dissolve in the mouth and trickle down the throat

Or try a glass of equal parts of white vinegar and warm water plus a teaspoon of salt. Stir till salt is dissolved, then gargle two teaspoons every twenty minutes.

Note: Do not swallow the gargle.

A level dessertspoon of white sugar soaked with brandy is also very good. Allow it to slowly trickle down your throat.

Sour Milk, Making Your Own

Simply add two tablespoons of white vinegar to one quart of fresh milk, shake or stir and that's it.

Spaghetti Squash, Cooking

Cut the squash in half, lengthwise, then steam it, cut side down, over one or two inches of water. After fifteen to twenty minutes, it's easy to scoop out the contents, in the form of long strings.

Note: Before steaming the squash, remove all seeds, but do not pare.

Splatters From Frying Meat, Preventing

Before heating the oil, sprinkle one half teaspoon of salt in the pan. Add the oil, and fry your meat with no splatters.

Sponges, Reviving

If they're looking faded and grimy, soak them overnight in a solution of two parts white vinegar and one part cold water. Next day, rinse them well in clean, cold water, then let them dry in the sunshine.

Spot Remover, Making Your Own

Mix together one part alcohol and two parts cold water. This solution is good on any fabric, particularly coloreds and acetates. Keep it in a bottle for instant use.

Squirrels, Keeping Them Away

Mix a box of moth balls crushed to a powder with equal parts of talcum powder. Sprinkle it around your attic and porch.

Or mix together two cups of flour, one ounce of tabasco sauce and one tablespoon of red pepper. Add enough water to make a thin paste. With a paintbrush, paint the trunk of the tree and the tops of the branches. It works.

Stamps, Removing From Envelopes

Simply put the whole envelope, or the piece with the stamp attached, in cold water for ten to fifteen minutes. It'll come off easily and won't lose its color.

Starching, Made Easy

To prevent your iron from sticking to the clothing, add a few drops of turpentine to the starching water and your iron will glide over the clothes.

Or add one half teaspoon of salt to the starch.

Or you can add one tablespoon of lard to the starch.

Also, if you want collars and cuffs stiff, it's a lot easier to starch them with liquid starch in an old roll-on deodorant bottle. Gently pry out the roll-on ball with a sharp knife or nail file, fill the bottle with liquid starch, press the ball back in, and presto just roll it onto the desired area.

Steak, Tenderizing

Rub both sides with pure lemon juice using the fingertips. Then do the same thing with olive oil. Allow it to stand for ten minutes, then place under the broiler or in the pan.

Steak Or Chops, Cooking

Never stick a fork in steaks or chops while cooking them, whether they're fried or grilled. That lets the juice out.

Stings

Apply a piece of soft cloth soaked in white vinegar to the spot. Hold it on until the pain stops.

Or rub honey onto the affected area. This is particularly good for bee stings.

Stockings, Silk

At first wearing, rub the toes and heels with a piece of beeswax. They'll last twice as long because the beeswax strengthens them.

Storing Whites Or Linens

Wrap them in blue tissue paper to prevent them from turning yellow.

Strawberries

If they're turning soft, just wash them in cold water, put them in a colander and let them stand in the refrigerator. They'll stay firm much longer.

Suede Coat, Cleaning

First, give it a good brushing with a suede brush, then wipe it completely with a piece of terry cloth that has been dipped in white vinegar, then wrung out until merely damp.

Any suede items, such as shoes, gloves, purses, can be cleaned using slightly stale bread. As the slice becomes soiled, change to another slice.

Sunburn, Relieving

Rub the burn with apple cider vinegar and pat on a very cold tea bag. If the burn is bad, make a paste of baking soda and white vinegar and pat it on the burn.

Suntan Lotion, Making Your Own

Mix together equal parts of sweet oil (odorless olive oil), brown vinegar, and cold brown tea. Put it in a spray bottle and give a good shake before spraying it on your skin.

Note: If you can't get sweet oil, ordinary olive oil will do.

Sweater, Drying It Quickly

Lay the sweater flat on a large beach towel, then lay another beach towel on top of the sweater. Roll it, pressing hard, with a rolling pin. You'll be surprised how much water comes out.

Sweeping Floors

Before sweeping your floors, give the bristles of your broom a good spray with furniture polish. Any dog or cat hairs, as well as lint and dirt, will cling to the broom. It makes sweeping much easier.

Sweet Potatoes, Dry Skins

To prevent the hard, leathery look and taste, rub each sweet potato with olive oil before baking.

Sweet Potatoes, Preventing Darkening

As you peel them, put them in a mixture of six teaspoons of salt and one quart of cold water.

Tablecloth, Plastic, Preserving

Pad the table itself with two or three sheets of newspaper under the plastic tablecloth. Cover the table completely, then fasten the newspaper under the edge of the table with thumbtacks or adhesive tape. The plastic tablecloth will last twice as long with the padding.

Note: If the plastic tablecloth is clear plastic, simply use white paper instead of newspaper for the same results.

Tablecloths, Preserving

To give them a much longer life, never fold them the same way after every washing. Fold them crosswise after every other ironing, and they'll last for a much longer period.

Tacks, Hammering

Force the tack through a small strip of cardboard to make it easy to hit and to avoid bruising your fingers.

Tar Stains On Material, Removing

Rub the spot with lard, then soak it in turpentine for five minutes. Scrape off the loosened tar and rinse in clean turpentine. Rub gently till dry.

Note: Don't use your dryer.

Or rub butter over the affected area, wait two minutes, then soak the material in gasoline. Work between the fingers, then wash by hand. Rinse well and dry it in the open air.

Note: Special precautions should be taken regarding fire.

If the fabric is corduroy, try using peanut butter. Work it into the stain, then wash in the normal way.

Or soak the corduroy in kerosene for fifteen minutes, then wash by hand.

Tea Stains, Removing
See Coffee And Tea Stains On Material, Removing

Tennis Shoes, Cleaning

Brush off as much dirt, mud, or grime as possible, then toss them into the washing machine, laces and all.

Note: When they are clean, put them out in the sun to dry.

Throat, Hoarse

Thoroughly beat together the white of an egg and one tablespoon of white sugar. Take it, slowly, just before retiring at night. Let it trickle down the throat.

Ticks On Dogs, Removing

Dip a cotton swab in pure alcohol and douse the tick attached to the skin. He'll let go in a few seconds. Pull it off and crush it immediately.

Or heat the tip of a needle and slowly force it through the front part of the tick. It'll let go quickly.

Tiles, Hearth Or Floor

Add two lumps, or two teaspoons, of sugar to the juice of a fresh lemon. With a soft cloth, apply the mixture to the dull area and keep rubbing till dry. Stains and dullness will disappear and the tiles will really shine.

Tin Utensils, Cleaning

Simply dip a rolled up ball of black and white newspaper in kerosene. Rub it hard over the tinware, then polish with a soft cloth.

Or lightly rub the tinware with half a raw potato dipped in baking soda.

Tinware, Preventing Rust

When tinware is new, rub it thoroughly inside and out with lard. Place it in the oven and heat it thoroughly. Tinware treated this way will last years longer.

Tobacco, Moistening And Sweetening

If your tobacco is hard, add some apple peel to the container. One or two inches is about normal for the average tobacco pouch and more can be added for larger containers.

Tobacco Smells In the House, Removing

One of the easiest ways is to mix one fourth cup of ammonia with one quart of cold water and let it stand overnight in the center of the room. Next morning all stale odors are gone.

Toilet Bowl Leaks

Put some liquid bluing in the toilet tank and don't flush the toilet for at least four hours. If the bluing appears in the toilet bowl, you need a new toilet tank valve. Testing for leaks saves high water bills.

Tomatoes, Keeping Them Fresh

Wash ripe tomatoes in a solution of one table-spoon of bleach to each quart of cold water. Dry with paper towels, then wrap individually in black and white newspaper.

Note: When ready to use, a quick rinse under the cold water tap removes all the bleach.

Tomato, Peeling

Place the tomato on the end of a fork and plunge it into boiling water for about ten seconds. The skin will burst and peel off like paper.

Tomato Blossoms, Falling Off

When this happens in the spring, lightly spray the ends of the vines, the flowered sections, with hair spray. A light coating will do.

Toothache

Oil of cloves is the best thing for a toothache. With the fingertip or cotton swab apply it directly onto the affected tooth and gum.

Or mix together a powder of one teaspoon of alum and two teaspoons of powdered cloves. Moisten a cotton swab, dip it in the powder and apply to the tooth.

Tortoise Shell, Cleaning

Wash it in warm, soapy water, then rinse and dry well. Moisten a cloth with linseed oil and apply. Polish it thoroughly.

Towels, Colors Running

Before washing them for the first time, if possible, soak the towels in a strong, salty, cold water solution for twenty-four hours.

Towels, Fading Or Stained
See Handkerchiefs And Towels, Bleaching

Trays, To Prevent Glasses From Slipping

Cover the tray with a small hand towel that's been dipped in cold water, then wrung out. Now, place the glasses on the towel and there will be no slippage at all.

Umbrella

Lightly scrub with a mixture of equal parts of warm water and ammonia. It'll not only clean it, but restores the color as well.

Umbrella Stand, Substitution

Place an ordinary sponge in a piece of heavy duty aluminum, then turn up the sides to make a box-like container.

Note: Be sure to remove and squeeze out the sponge from time to time.

Unpainted Furniture, Cleaning

Dust first, then clean with a dampened soft cloth, sprinkled with fine sand or baking soda.

Upholstery, Cleaning

Mix together one cup of soap flakes or three fourths cup of liquid detergent with two cups of boiling water. Allow it to cool slightly, then, as it turns to jelly, whip it into a stiff lather. Apply it to the upholstery with a nail brush. Clean as necessary, then wipe off with a soft cloth dampened with white vinegar.

Vacuum Cleaner, Emptying

When you spread out the newspaper, prior to emptying the vacuum cleaner bag onto it, lightly sprinkle the paper with cold water.

Vases, Narrow Necked, Cleaning

To clean them easily, fill the vase with lukewarm water, then drop in a denture cleaning tablet. Wait ten minutes, shake vigorously, then wash and rinse in warm water and white vinegar.

Vases Leaking

Simply melt some paraffin and pour it inside the vase. Roll it around so that the paraffin coats completely, then let it stand till the paraffin turns cold.

Vegetables, Bringing Out the Flavor

A teaspoon of white sugar added to the vegetable water gives any vegetable a really natural taste. Use just enough water to cover the vegetables. That way you'll save the vitamins and minerals.

Vegetables And Greens

Any vegetable in your refrigerator will keep twice as long if you line the bottom of the refrigerator with paper towels. They absorb the moisture that ruins most fruits and vegetables.

Note: Change the paper toweling once a week.

Vegetable Odors, When Cooking Greens

Add two teaspoons of vinegar or two teaspoons of sugar to the water to prevent odors in your kitchen.

Or put one half a pint of vinegar in a large saucepan on the stove. No heat is necessary, just let it stand there while you are cooking your vegetables.

Vegetable Stains, Removing

Rub the stain with a slice of fresh, raw potato. Let dry, then wash the normal way.

Velvet, Cleaning

The best method is to hold a steam iron about two inches from the material and steam for about two to three minutes. While steaming, wipe the velvet with a soft piece of cloth. Then use a nail brush to gently brush against the grain.

Vinyl Upholstery, Cleaning

Never use oils to clean vinyl upholstery. It often hardens the vinyl. The best thing to use is two tablespoons of any mild liquid detergent in one pint of tepid water. A good rubbing and then another wipe and polish should do it.

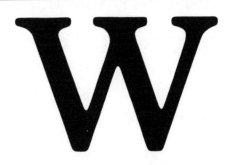

Waffles, Sticking

If you're sure the mixture, heat setting and other variables are okay, yet the waffles are still sticking, it's probably because there is not enough oil in the mixture. Try adding another teaspoon. It often makes the difference.

Wallet Protector

If you're prone to losing your wallet, try this. Open it up, lay it flat, then wrap a rubber band around each half. Fold it and return it to your pocket and there will be no more slips.

Wallpaper, Cleaning

Dust it thoroughly with a soft cloth, then rub it with a piece of bread (not too fresh or too stale). Rub evenly and change the bread as it becomes soiled.

Wallpaper, Removing

Mix two tablespoons of saltpeter into one gallon of very hot water. When dissolved, apply the mixture freely to the wallpaper. After a few minutes, the wallpaper should come off easily. You can put a few slits in the paper with a knife blade.

Note: Put towels or newspaper on the floor to prevent damage to your carpets, rugs, or flooring.

Walnuts, Cracking

Soak the entire nut in cold, salty water (three cups of salt to each gallon of water), overnight. Next morning, they'll crack very easily.

Warts, Removing

First thing every morning, upon waking, rub the ends of three fingers (one at a time) on your tongue, then rub it directly on the wart. Wait five minutes, then start your regular cleanup. Do this every morning for three weeks and the wart will disappear.

Note: The accumulated acids on your tongue are the reason for the cure. Also, to help you remember, put something different beside your bed each night (an overturned glass, soup plate, spoon). It works.

The milk (white) from a fig leaf applied regularly is also very good.

Wasps, Getting Rid Of

When you see the wasp entering its nest, give your can of hairspray a good shake, then spray directly into the wasp nest hole. The spray coats the wings so the wasp can't fly.

Watermelon, Freezing

After cutting the melon into one inch squares (no skin, seeds, or white), lay the pieces on a cookie sheet (not touching) and freeze for forty-five minutes. Remove them from the freezer. They'll keep for twelve months.

Note: Cantaloupe can be frozen the same way.

Water Pipes, Frozen

Quite often a hair dryer set on hot will do the trick.

Or turn the faucet upside down, using a wrench or pliers. Then pour some very salty, boiling water down the pipe.

Washing Machine, Cleaning The Interior

To get rid of a buildup of soap scum and lint, pour one gallon of white vinegar into the empty machine. Fill with warm water and run through the entire cycle. You'll be amazed at the results.

Wax Fruit, Cleaning

Simply wipe it with a cloth moistened with alcohol.

To clean wax flowers, dip them in alcohol and scrub them with an old toothbrush.

Weeds, Killing

Spray with a mixture of hot, very salty water. If weeds are growing among plants, pour the water directly onto the weed and around the base.

Weevils, Getting Rid Of

Fill some ordinary bottle caps from ketchup or soft drink bottles with crushed red peppers, and place them at various points in your cupboard. They hate the smell and quickly disappear.

Whole bay leaves are another good weevil chaser. Scatter them around your cupboards, as well as putting one or two in your flour containers, cereal boxes and other containers.

Whipped Cream

Add a teaspoon of honey to the cream and it'll stay firm in cakes, cookies, etc.

Whites, Fading

Boil fading whites in two gallons of water to which one half cup of cream of tartar has been added.

If linen is fading or turning yellow soak it in buttermilk for twenty minutes, then rinse well and hang out to dry in the sunshine.

Whites, Keeping Them White

Soak them in hot water to which you've added one teaspoon of peroxide for each gallon of water.

Or slice up a fresh onion and boil it with the water in which you've placed your whites.

A teaspoonful of turpentine, boiled with the clothes, is another way of keeping them snowy white.

Wicker Furniture, Brown, Cleaning

After a good dusting, wash with warm water, then rinse with warm, salty water. Dry thoroughly. Polish with furniture polish, then set it out in the open air.

Give it a good oiling, by rubbing it with a soft cloth dampened with lemon oil. It'll prevent it from cracking and splitting in the future.

Windows, Cleaning

If windows are very dirty, wipe them with a cloth dampened with warm water, then wipe again with second cloth soaked in methylated spirits. No polishing is required. Or add vinegar to the water to produce a brilliant polish.

Note: Never use soap on windows. It leaves a film.

Another method is to fill a sixteen ounce spray bottle with four tablespoons of ammonia, one tablespoon of white vinegar and cool water. Shake and spray. It's as good as any you'll buy.

Windows, Cleaning In Freezing Weather

Wash them with a soft cloth soaked in a mixture of one fourth cup of denatured alcohol and one quart of warm water. Polish with an old black and white newspaper.

Windows, Cracked, Repairing

Until it can be replaced, the best thing to use is a coating of clear white shellac. Paint both the inside and outside, and it'll do the job.

Windows, Frosting Up

Rub either alcohol or cold, salty water on the outside of your windows, then polish with crumpled black and white newspaper.

Windows, Sticking

Rub the window slides with either floor wax or candle wax. They'll slide much easier, even in cold weather.

Or coat the window slides with melted Vaseline or petroleum jelly. Simply warm it by putting in hot water for a few seconds, then apply with the fingertips.

Window Blinds

Dust, clean, and freshen them with a cloth moistened with linseed oil.

Window Boxes

To save your soil and prevent nasty black stains from splattering, cover the top of your soil with a thin layer of small pebbles or gravel.

Wine Stains, Removing

If possible, hold the stained cloth in boiling milk. After a minute or so, the stain will disappear.

Wire Screens, Cleaning

First, brush the screen thoroughly with a broom or brush to remove dust. Using a nail brush, scrub with pure kerosene. Be sure to do the corners and edges as well; this is where most rust starts. Scrub both sides of the wire for best results.

Wire Screen, Repairing

If it is a small hole, clear nail polish applied with a cotton swab will seal the hole quickly.

If it is a large hole, cut out a piece of wire screen to cover the hole, then stick it on with airplane glue. It helps to weave the edge of the patch onto the screen before applying the glue.

Wooden Dishes, Repairing

Never use soap. Clean them with fine sand, applied with a damp cloth moistened with white vinegar. Rub in a circular motion, then rinse well and, if possible, let dry in the open air.

Wooden Floors, Cleaning

Never use plain water. The best thing to use is kerosene. Go over the floor with a soft cloth dampened with kerosene, then polish with a second cloth.

Note: A good polisher is a large piece of soft cloth, soaked in kerosene, then dried in the sun. It gives a marvelous polish.

Wooden Floors, Losing Their Color

Make tea to match the color of your floor, for instance, very dark, medium, or lightly stained. When tea is cold, apply it to the faded area with a soft white cloth. When dry, wax or polish in the usual way.

Note: Cold tea is also very good as a cleaner.

Wooden Floors, Squeaking

A generous amount of liquid wax poured into the cracks usually does the job.

Talcum powder or powdered graphite often stops the squeaks.

Wooden Spoons And Cutting Boards, Rough

Smooth them by rubbing with fine sandpaper with the grain. When smooth, wash and rinse in cold water.

Woodwork, White, Cleaning

Wash white woodwork with a soft cloth soaked in warm, soapy water. If it is stained, crush a couple of egg shells into a powder and lightly scrub with a small brush. Rinse with a mixture of white vinegar and warm water, then polish with a piece of flannel.

Woodwork Scratches, Removing

Rub the scratch with a slice of fresh lemon. This often works wonders.

Woolens, Storing

Crush about a dozen moth balls to a powder and dissolve them in the final rinse water to keep the moths away.

Also, after rinsing and drying, wrap them in white or blue tissue paper, then wrap them again in black and white newspaper.

Yeast

Bury the yeast cake in household salt and it will keep for a long time.

Zinc, Cleaning

Make a paste of lime and water, apply, rub hard, then polish with a soft cloth.

Zipper, Stuck Or Hard To Operate

Simply take a lead pencil and rub the lead up and down the zipper, making sure you cover the teeth. The graphite in the lead will have it operating smoothly in no time.

Or rub a candle on the teeth of the zipper to make it much easier to operate.

Chuck (Charles Stephen) Faulkner III was born in Ireland, raised in Australia, and is now a resident of Norfolk, Virginia. He hosts a call-in radio show on WNIS AM in Tidewater four hours every weeknight, and a one-hour "Ask Your Neighbor" show every Friday evening. Mr. Faulkner has conducted the "ask your neighbor" format in many cities over the years, collecting a vast array of recipes, household hints, and just plain common sense which goes back to Ireland and Australia. The winner of many awards in radio, television, and film, he is now appearing every weekday on the Continental Broadcasting Network's show "Time Out," where he does a five-minute spot called "The Hint Man."